Global History

A View from the South

Samir Amin

Pambazuka Press
An imprint of Fahamu

CODESRIA

BOOKS *for* CHANGE
Dedicated to Development
International Publishing House

Published 2011 by Pambazuka Press, an imprint of Fahamu
Cape Town, Dakar, Nairobi and Oxford
www.pambazukapress.org www.fahamubooks.org www.pambazuka.org

CODESRIA
Dakar
www.codesria.org

and

Books *for* Change,
Bangalore
www.booksforchange.info

Fahamu, 2nd floor, 51 Cornmarket Street, Oxford OX1 3HA, UK
Fahamu Kenya, PO Box 47158, 00100 GPO, Nairobi, Kenya
Fahamu Senegal, 9 Cité Sonatel 2, POB 25021, Dakar-Fann, Dakar, Senegal
Fahamu South Africa, c/o 19 Nerina Crescent, Fish Hoek,
7975 Cape Town, South Africa

CODESRIA, Avenue Cheikh Anta Diop X Canal IV, BP 3304, CP 18524,
Dakar, Senegal

Books *for* Change, 139 Richmond Road, Bangalore 560 025, India

The Introduction and Chapters 2, 5 and 6 were translated
by Victoria Bawtree.

British Library Cataloguing in Publication Data
A catalogue record for this book is available from the British Library

ISBN: 978-1-906387-96-9 paperback
ISBN: 978-1-906387-97-6 ebook – pdf
ISBN India: 978-81-8291-110-9

Printed on demand by Lightning Source

Contents

 **Introduction**

This book brings together various contributions I have written for the elaboration of a global history. They have been published in French and English in different periodicals and on different dates, some of them a while ago.[1] Their collection into one volume highlights their originality. First, because this enables the reader to identify precisely the theses that I put forward in my early critique of 'Eurocentric' history (see my book *Eurocentrism*, 1989), which still predominates the 'modern' capitalist ideology that shapes contemporary social thought. And, second, because I propose to treat these 'questions of the past' not as separate from the challenges of the present or from the alternatives for possible futures, including, indeed, the question of a 'socialism for the 21st century'.

I was an early reader of Marx. I very carefully read *Capital* and the other works by Marx and Engels that were available in French during my university studies between 1948 and 1955. I also decided to read the authors who were criticised by Marx (including Smith, Ricardo, Bastiat and Say). All this certainly gave me the utmost intellectual pleasure and convinced me of the power of Marx's thought. But at the same time, I remained unsatisfied. For I had posed one central question, that of the 'under-development' (a new term beginning to be widely used) of the societies of contemporary Asia and Africa, for which I had found no answers in Marx. The texts that were published for the first time in French in 1960, the *Grundrisse*, also left me unsatisfied.

Far from 'abandoning' Marx, and judging that he had been supplanted, I simply concluded that his work had remained unfinished. Marx never completed the work he had intended to do, including, among other things, integrating the 'world dimension' of capitalism into his analysis and systematically articulating the question of power (politics) and the economy (capitalist and pre-capitalist). All we have are some brilliant observations on these subjects in his treatment of the French revolutions (from the Great Revolution to the Paris Commune of 1871 and not forgetting 1848).

1

GLOBAL HISTORY: A VIEW FROM THE SOUTH

The question of the (unequal) 'development' that is characteristic of globalised capitalism thus led me, since my university studies, to concentrate on the first of these dimensions, as testified by my doctoral thesis ('L'accumulation à l'échelle mondiale') in 1957. For me this was a starting point, a first stage in the work that I pursued over the following 50 years. I will not retrace the successive stages of this development. But I think it is useful to call attention to the whole question of 'unequal development' that I proposed in 1973, in a book with this title, and to two other works written in the same period, *The Law of Value and Historical Materialism* (1978) and 'L'échange inégal et la loi de la valeur' (1973[1977]).

To arrive at this formulation I decided to do further study in these two fields, inspired by the wonderful lesson on them that Marx himself had given us. First, I delved into a careful reading of the great works of vulgar[2] economics after Marx, in response to Marx, as Marx had taught us we should do by his criticism of 'classic' economics and its first vulgar derivations. This involved a direct reading of the work of Böhm-Bawerk, Walras and the other producers of the fundaments of the new 'subjective' economics, up to the formulations of Keynes and Sraffa. I already proposed such a critical reading in the first French edition of *L'Accumulation à l'echelle mondiale* (1957), then took it up again in 'L'échange inégal'. To read Marx today – that is, after Marx — entails this critical reading which convinced me of the vulgar and ideological (in the functional sense of the word) character of the new bourgeois economics, post and anti-Marxist.

Marx did not limit himself to the theoretical criticism of his precursors. At the same time he opposed them by an orderly presentation of an immense amount of empirical facts. So I thought that it was not enough to criticise post-Marx bourgeois economics: the task also had to be completed by an orderly presentation of the 'facts' that illustrate how globalised capitalism really works. I made a first collection of this mass of empirical data in *L'Accumulation*; I then updated it for my publications in the 1970s. I continued this work, looking more closely at what was going on at the time. The first – 'Awakening of the South' (2008) – was represented by the Bandung period (1955–1981). Those who read my writings carefully – mainly the British and the Japanese – took note of these 'empirical studies'.

What followed was related to two sets of issues: first, the so-called development economics and second, markets (and the role of expectations), which I intended to analyse in depth.

The first of these seemed to me rather poor on the whole, incapable of moving forward from the obligatory vision of the 'unavoidable stages of development'. I had already formulated a radical critique of this mechanistic and vulgar vision three years before Rostow himself presented it in his 1960 book (*The Stages of Economic Growth: A Non-Communist Manifesto*). But since then 'development economics', preached by the main institutions responsible for development interventions (the World Bank, cooperation programmes, universities), have never gone beyond this nonsense.

As for the second, I felt it was continuing the vulgar drift, taking it to its logical extreme: the construction of an 'imaginary economy' – that of generalised markets – which had no relationship whatever with actually existing capitalism. The centrality of the empty and unreal concept of 'expectations' that was necessary for this construction, completed the drift. Economic theory became a scholastic text dedicated to discussing something like the 'sex of angels' with the idea, like that of their predecessors in the Middle Ages, that the answer to this question was the best way of understanding the world. At the same time, this drift, which claimed to be empirical, aimed at integrating into its theses an increasing, but disorderly, mass of empirical data. The mathematical method that this treatment involves is certainly not to be rejected in itself. But the continual sophistication of its method does not eliminate the absurd – unreal – character of the questions that its users pose: the 'anticipations' (the sex of angels).

Nevertheless, neither my criticism of vulgar theory and its pseudo-empirical applications, nor my counter proposals suggesting that the mass of orderly data be integrated into a theory of actually existing capitalism, seemed enough to understand the whole reality of unequal development. Articulating the political/ideological/cultural dimensions with that of the economic management of society: this was, I thought, the main theme of a historical materialist interpretation that could not be avoided. And in this field, my reading of Marx had already convinced me that my first propositions should be taken further. This I tried to do by putting forward both a general concept of the tributary mode of production based on the great family of the organisations of pre-capitalist advanced class societies, contrasting their articulation of the dominant power and the dominated economy, to its opposite, which was particular to capitalism. From this I drew some important conclusions concerning the forms of alienation particular to ancient societies as well as to modern capitalist society. I also sought to identify, in the various tributary forms, the concrete contradictions at work that could accelerate or delay the capitalist advance. Then I tried to integrate the questions posed in terms of historical materialism and those that concerned the economic dimension, as could be seen by the readers of *Unequal Development* and *The Law of Value and Historical Materialism*.

My work has never been that of a Marxologue.[3] I have repeated many times that, for me, to be a Marxist is to start from Marx and not to stop with him, or with his main successors (Lenin, Mao), the builders of historical Marxism.

The most important of my conclusions was the formulation of a 'law of globalised value' which is consistent with the essentials of the law of value particular to capitalism and discovered by Marx on the one hand, and with the realities of an unequal globalised development on the other. My main contribution concerns the study of the passing from the law of value to the law of globalised value, based on the hierarchisation – itself globalised – of the price of labour around its value. Together with the management practices concerning the access to natural resources, this globalisation of value is the basis of the 'imperialist rent'.[4] It is my view that this was responsible for the major contradictions of actually existing capitalism/imperialism and the conflicts associated with them, so that classes and nations are interlinked in their struggles and conflicts, in all the complexity of their specific and concrete articulations. I believe that a study of the 20th and 21st centuries must necessarily lead to the emergence – or the awakening – of the peoples and nations of the peripheries of the globalised capitalist/imperialist system.

I have therefore refused the two versions of the main concept proposed by historical Marxisms concerning global history, both of them based on what is claimed to be a definitive formulation of historical materialism: the version that constricted this history in the straitjacket of the 'five universal stages' (primitive commu-nism, slavery, feudalism, capitalism, socialism) and the one that contrasted the two paths (European and Asian). Instead of this I proposed, as from 1970, considering a succession of three great stages (communitarian, tributary – a term widely adopted since then – and capitalist), the forms of each of the first two stages hav-ing been multiple (thus relativising the form of European feudal-ism in the great tributary family).

Similar contradictions riddled all the societies of the tributary age, for which a positive solution involved the invention of the principles of a more advanced stage of universal civilisation (that of capitalist modernity). These responses to the challenge were expressed in successive waves that gradually invented modernity, moving from the East to the West, from China of the Sōng to the Arab-Persian Abbassid Caliphate, then to the Italian towns, before finding its European form that took shape during the 16th century in the London–Amsterdam–Paris triangle. This last form pro-duced historical capitalism, which has imposed itself through its conquest of the world, annihilating the previous variants which could have been possible and were both similar and different from the one we know. This conquest of the world by European capitalism is at the origin of Eurocentric interpretations of global history and, among others, the two versions of historical material-ism of the historical Marxisms that I have criticised. My analysis emphasises the qualitative transformation that mainly defined each of the three great stages. It particularly stresses the reversal of the relationships between the economic instance (always deter-minant 'in the last resort') and the politico-ideological instance that was directly dominant in the family of tributary systems (European feudalism included), which is now subordinated to the direct domination of the economic instance in capitalism.

This, at all events, is how I read Marx and the fundamental critique that he developed in *Capital*. This is the reason why I con-sider that it is the 'economistic' alienation particular to capitalism that gives modern civilisation its essential character. In contrast, all the societies of the tributary era were characterised by another form of alienation, necessary to affirm the direct dominance by the political instance. The religious or para-religious variants of this alienation, which were different from the economistic alienation, were especially appropriate for the requirements of the tributary era civilisations.

In my view, capitalism did not achieve its completed form until after its double revolution. It was, on the one hand, a political revolution that affirmed the decisive power of the bourgeoisie (in successive forms, from the not very glorious English revolution in 1688, the war of independence of the United States, but above all the French revolution that inaugurated modern politics) and, on the other hand, an industrial revolution that, through the activities of 'great industry' (at the beginning of the 19th century) led to the domination of economics and the capitalist economistic alienation through which it is expressed.

Most North American authors of global history have doubted the importance, even the reality, of the Industrial Revolution and have reduced it to the level of 'industrious' revolutions which, from China of ancient times to the early Middle Ages in Europe, as well as in the Middle East and Italian towns, shaped the cycles of advances (often followed by retreats) of the civilisations of the tributary epoch. Calling these industrious revolutions, which were almost always associated with expansion of wage labour, commercial relationships and even free thought, the 'beginnings of capitalism' does not upset me. Conflating these with capitalism itself results in obfuscating the complete rupture that capitalism represents with previous forms of industrialisation.

For Europe between 1500 to 1800, I consider that the Ancien Régime and mercantilism kept their character of a 'transition to capitalism', as shown by the dispute for power between the old tributary governing class (the 'feudal' aristocracy) and the budding bourgeoisie (almost exclusively commercial, sometimes financial, often supported by part of the peasantry and the landed aristocracy that was transforming itself into a class of capitalist farmers). It was also characterised by the conflict between the domination of the political instance (marked by the absolute monarchy, when it was the instrument of an enlightened despotism) and that of the new economic instance.

The global history that I have proposed has led me to conclusions that I feel are important. Most of the authors of global history remain ignorant of them. Capitalism is, in this interpretation, a system that is qualitatively new (and 'superior', I dare to say), the incubation of which stretched over a long period of time, at least seven centuries, from the Chinese epoch of the Sōng to European Atlantic mercantilism. The difference between the Eurocentric viewpoint and my rejection of it is to be found precisely in the analysis of this long incubation. For the Eurocentrics, the incubation concerns only Europe (between 1500 and 1800) and capitalism then appears as the result of the European exception: the European 'miracle' (see my critique in *Eurocentrism* (1989) of this modern ideology, which only took form after the triumph of completed capitalism in the 19th century, but still endures today).

I believe that this incubation is expressed through waves of successive advances that occurred over centuries in different regions of the eastern hemisphere – Eurasia and Africa. From them arose the same fundamental contradictions typical of tributary systems, as I have already pointed out. That capitalism could have been 'born' elsewhere than in Europe, and for this reason have both similar and different characteristics than that of completed historical capitalism ('European'), so be it. But the task of history analysts is not to imagine possible different evolutions that did not occur, but to explain those that did. I explained the late success (but rapid maturation) of the Euro-Atlantic form, by the peripheral character of the feudal mode and its coincidence with another major fact in history: the conquest of the Americas.

My book, *The Law of Value and Historical Materialism* (1978) – which is in the process of being revised and republished – stresses the unavoidable detour through the value (and the economic alienation motivating it) that is ignored by the empirical approach in terms of 'observed prices' (very few of the writers of global history go beyond this empirical horizon). I put as much emphasis on the centre/periphery contrast in the typical forms of historical capitalism (European by origin). There was a qualitatively different contrast from that which characterised the relationships between the centres and peripheries of the old times. The use of the same terms for analysing the systems of different epochs obviously runs the risk of a shift toward an affirmation of the analogy, which is superficial, if not false in my opinion. I therefore found myself almost alone, with Giovanni Arrighi, having analysed the contrast in terms of a globalisation of the law of value based on accumulation by dispossession which produced a growing and insuperable conflict in the framework of the workings of capitalist logic between the dominant imperialist centres and the dominated peripheries.

It is therefore not by chance that it is precisely on this question that my analysis – that I claim to make within the fundamental critical analysis of society started by Marx – departs from those put forward by most of the contemporary schools of global history.

Some – Wallerstein in particular – admit, like myself, that capitalist modernity has created a civilisation that is qualitatively different from that which preceded it. But the definition that Wallerstein gives to capitalism ignores economic alienation, which is central for me, as it was, I think, for Marx. Other schools of global history deny outright all validity of the emphasis on the qualitative transformation, replacing it by a continuous vision of a permanent, quantitatively growing accumulation. Many of these works – which are in fact remarkable – thus stress the commercial exchanges and transfers of technological and institutional knowledge, like religious beliefs and cultural habits, and underline, in this respect, the previous contributions of the Easterners to the late invention of European capitalism. André Gunder Frank joined this current of thinking in his book *ReORIENT: Global Economy in the Asian Age*. My thesis concerning the successive waves of inventions of capitalist modernity integrates the contribution of the work of these schools of global history but, I believe, enriches them by stressing the qualitative leap that took place.

The North American schools of global history do not distinguish between commercial relationships and capitalist commercial relationships. The equation for commercial exchanges ($M + E = M1$) reminds us that the gain (then improperly described as accumulation) is the result of a trade in goods, which have been produced in the framework of non-capitalist production relationships, by peasants or by artisans, even if they have been, in certain circumstances, subordinated and dominated by commercial capital and even when the organisation of production used waged workers. In the equation $M + P = M1$, P stands for the production organised in the framework of social relationships specific to capitalism: ownership of the means of production (modern: the factory), separated from the producers (wage labourers, sellers of their labour power). Without these relationships there is neither capital (which is constituted by social relationships, not reducible to the 'thing' which represents them: the equipment), nor surplus value shared between wages and profits nor, strictly speaking, capitalist commercial alienation (wages seem to constitute the price of labour when it is the price of the workforce and, logically, capital itself seems to be productive), nor the accumulation of capital. This confusion makes it difficult to do justice to the qualitative transformation of society that took place with the Industrial Revolution of the 19th century. Of course, these transformations did not spring out of nowhere, but were the result of a long incubation prepared by some ten centuries of expansion of the spheres of commercial exchanges (which were often followed by contractions). These certainly led to proto-capitalist relationships here and there (but not always) and they certainly led to the invention of an advanced range of the tools essential to the birth of capitalism: credit, particularly, homogenising globalisation (or rather regionalisation, in fact), monetary instruments, trade. But these beginnings by themselves alone did not constitute a system of capitalist social relationships.

Wallerstein still accepts the validity of considering the qualitative transformation represented by capitalist modernity, even if his definition of capitalism remains descriptive and incomplete. It is not therefore surprising that other theoreticians of global history and the economic world (for example, André Gunder Frank in his later works) have renounced outright giving any significance to the concept of the mode of production and have spoken of 'capitalism' that existed since the birth of humankind.

In contrast, all these – considerable – contributions of the schools of global history are perfectly consistent with their 'Marxist' interpretation, formulated in terms of the expression of the internal contradictions which were typical of what I have described as the family of tributary formations producing the 'inventions' associated with the commercial expansions that prepared their coming together into the new capitalist mode of production.

The theses that I have developed on global history never seemed to me to require the abandonment of Marxism. On the contrary, it was by starting from Marx that it has been possible for me to get out of the empirical rut in which a good number of writers about global history have remained bogged down. I even dare to claim that this attitude, which starts from Marx and does not hesitate to develop and enrich the historical materialism method begun – but only begun – by Marx, is the only way of advancing the analyses of global history.

It is understandable that serious historians have tired of Church Marxisms and their exegeses of the sacred texts of the Master, such as the Marxisms of the apparatchiks, concerned to justify by any means (honest or less honest) the daily requirements of their stand when faced with the challenge described above (but which is never recognised as such). But these historians have thrown the baby (Marx) out with the bathwater (historical Marxisms). By refusing to yield to this mood of the times, I think I have chosen the most fertile ground for analysis and action. It is for the reader to judge this from my contributions here to the debates concerning global history.

Right from the beginning (my doctoral thesis) I had adopted a twofold viewpoint that was deliberately globalist (as in today's jargon of global history) and a radical critique of Eurocentrism. I tried to put forward Marxist analyses forming part of this line of thinking and which were therefore critical of those of historical Marxisms (particularly those of the 'five stages' and those of the 'two paths, European and Asian'). Towards the end of the 1960s we therefore naturally met together – André Gunder Frank, Giovanni Arrighi, Immanuel Wallerstein and myself – as we shared this general viewpoint. It was thus not by chance that this 'gang of four', as we were later to be called, produced some works together which I believe were in advance of their time. We proposed an analysis of the long crisis which began in the 1970s (and from which the world has not yet extricated itself!), seen as a crisis of capitalist globalisation. This basic convergence did not of course exclude the diversity of our approaches, which were more complementary than contradictory. Some of these divergences became more marked, as can be seen from my criticism of *ReORIENT*, which appears in Chapter 4 of this book.

For this collection I have chosen articles that emphasised the unequalled power of Marx's method (not necessarily that of the historical Marxisms) in the analysis of global history. The viewpoint is that of an Afro-Asian observer. My publications in Arabic, the translation of my works in numerous languages, particularly into Chinese and Arabic, have facilitated the widening of the debate so that it has left the US academic world behind, as well as the belated efforts of their European imitators.

Note

1. Chapter 1 was first published in 1991 as 'The ancient world systems versus the modern capitalist world system', *Review*, vol. XIV, no. 3, pp. 349–85; Chapter 2 in 1996 as 'Le role de l'Asie centrale dans le système tributaire de l'ancien monde' in *Les défis de la mondialisation*, Paris, Harmattan; Chapter 3 in 1996 as 'The challenge of globalisation', *Review of International Political Economy*, vol. 3, no. 2, pp. 216–59; Chapter 4 in 1999 as 'History conceived as an eternal cycle', *Review*, vol. XXII, no. 3, pp. 291–326; and Chapter 6 in 1998 as 'La Russie dans le système mondial', in *Review*, vol. XXI, no. 2, pp. 207–219.
2. In this book the word 'vulgar' is used in its Marxist sense of banal, populist or lacking in intellectual rigour.
3. A 'Marxalogue' is one who writes 'marxology', i.e. the critical interpretation of Marx's writings.
4. 'Monopoly rent' was defined by Marx as the difference between the price of production and market price where market price is set not by the average profit that results from equalisation of the rate of profits over time; instead the price is set by a few cartels or corporations. In the current imperialist epoch, a small number of oligopolies sets the world prices in various sectors of production (e.g. oil, medicines, biotechnology, agricultural inputs), and thus monopoly rent is often referred to as imperialist rent or rent of oligopolies. Where finance capital exercises the same control over prices, the term financialised monopoly rent is sometimes used.

References

Amin, Samir (1957[1974]) *Accumulation on a World Scale: A Critique of the Theory of Underdevelopment*, New York, NY, Monthly Review Press
——(1973) 'L'échange inégal et la loi de la valeur', *Anthropos*; English translation available in Amin, S. (1977) *Imperialism and Unequal Development*, New York, NY, Monthly Review Press
——(1978) *The Law of Value and Historical Materialism*, New York, NY, Monthly Review Press
——(1996) *Les défis de la mondialisation*, Harmattan, Paris
——(2008) *L'éveil du Sud*, Le Temps des Cerises, Paris (no English translation available; in English the title would read *The Awakening of the South*)
——(2010) *Eurocentrism* 2nd edition, Oxford, Pambazuka Press
Frank, André Gunder (1998) *ReORIENT: Global Economy in the Asian Age*, Berkeley, CA, University of California Press

1

The ancient world systems versus the modern capitalist world system

The modern world has produced a general image of universal history founded on the proposition that (European) capitalism is the first social system to unify the world. The least that can be said in that respect is that this statement seriously distorts reality and – I submit – is basically an expression of the dominant Eurocentric ideology. In fact, societies prior to the 16th century were in no way isolated from one another but were competitive partners within at least regional systems (and perhaps even a world system). Overlooking their interaction, one can hardly understand the dynamics of their evolution.

Simultaneously, I maintain that capitalism is a qualitatively new age in universal history which started around 1500. Therefore I insist upon distinguishing the modern capitalist overall structure from protocapitalist elements which indeed appeared in previous societies, sometimes since quite ancient times; I also insist upon the specificity of the capitalist centre/periphery dichotomy *vis-à-vis* previous forms of polarisation.

The specificity of capitalism *vis-à-vis* previous social formations

The theoretical contribution of the Marxist concept of the capitalist mode of production is crucial to this discussion. Its eventual dilution (fashionable nowadays of course) does not help clarify the issues. The capitalist mode of productions entails private ownership of the means of production which are themselves the product of labour, namely machinery. This in turn presumes a higher level of development of the forces of production (compared to the artisan and his instruments) and, on this basis, the division of society into two fundamental classes. Correspondingly, socially necessary labour takes the form of free wage labour. The generalised capitalist market thus constitutes the framework in which economic laws ('competition') operate as forces independent of subjective will. Economistic alienation and the dominance of economics are its expression.

No society prior to modern times was based on such principles. All advanced societies from 300 BC to 1500 AD were, from one end of the period to the other, of a profoundly similar nature, which I call tributary in order to show this essential *qualitative* fact: namely, that the surplus is directly tapped from peasant activity through some transparent devices associated with the organisation of the power hierarchy (power is the source of wealth, while in capitalism the opposite is the rule). The reproduction of the system therefore requires the dominance of an ideology – a state religion – which renders opaque the power organisation and legitimises it (in contrast to the economist ideology of capitalism which makes economic exploitation opaque and justifies it through this means, counterbalancing the relative openness of political relations, itself a condition for the emergence of modern democracy).

Having taken a stand on some of the debates of historical materialism, I believe it helpful to recall my essential conclusions. They affect my suggestions on the nature of the one (or more) pre-modern system(s). I have rejected the supposedly Marxist version of five stages. More precisely I refuse: (1) to regard slavery as a necessary stage through which all societies that are more 'advanced' have passed; (2) to regard feudalism as the necessary stage succeeding slavery. I have also rejected the supposedly Marxist version of the two roads. More precisely, I refuse to consider that only the European road (slavery-to-feudalism) would pave the way to the invention of capitalism, while the Asiatic road (the supposed Asiatic mode of production) would constitute an impasse, incapable of evolving by itself. I have described these two interpretations of historical materialism as products of Eurocentrism. I refer to my alternative suggestions in *Class and Nation*. I suggested the necessary succession of two families of modes of production: the communal family and the tributary family. This suggestion comes from highlighting two qualitative breaks in the general evolution: (1) later in date: the qualitative break from the dominance of the political and ideological instance (state plus metaphysical ideology) in the tributary phase into the dominance of the economic instance (generalised market and economistic ideology) in the capitalist phase; (2) previously: the qualitative break from the absence of a state and the dominance of the ideology of kinship in the communal phase into the crystallisation of social power in the statist-ideological-metaphysical form in the tributary phase, with precisely the description of feudalism as a peripheral tributary form.

To some, the forms I call 'tributary' would not constitute a single mode of production in the sense that they believe Marxism attaches to the concept of the mode of production. I shall not indulge in this kind of Marxology. If it is a nuisance I am ready to replace the term 'tributary mode of production' with the broader expression 'tributary society'. Of course my suggestions remain within a framework dominated by the search for general laws. Include in this, on the basis of these conceptualisations I have suggested, their transition towards capitalism, marked by the development of the protocapitalist elements which appeared earlier in history. There is of course a strong current nowadays rejecting any search for general laws and insisting on the irreducible specificity of various evolutionary paths. I take this epistemological orientation to be a product of a Eurocentrism concerned above all with legitimatising the superiority of the West.

The specificity of the capitalist world system

The first question the debate on this subject encounters concerns the character of worldwide capitalist expansion. For my part, along with others (including A.G. Frank), I hold that the processes governing the system as a whole determine the framework in which local adjustments operate. In other words, this systemic approach makes the distinction between external factors and internal factors relative, since all the factors are internal at the level of the world system. Is there any need to stress that this methodological approach is distinct from prevailing (bourgeois and even current Marxist) approaches? According to the latter, internal factors are decisive in the sense that the specificities of each ('developed' or 'undeveloped') national formation are mainly due to internal factors, whether favourable or unfavourable to capitalist development.

My analysis remains broadly based on a qualitative distinction (decisive in my view) between the societies of capitalism, dominated by economics (the law of value), and previous societies dominated by the political and ideological. There is, as I see it, a fundamental difference between the contemporary (capitalist) world system and all the preceding (regional and tributary) systems. This calls for comment on the law of value governing capitalism.

On that ground, I have expressed my point of view in terms of what I have called 'the worldwide expansion of the capitalist law of value'. Generally speaking, the law of value supposes an integrated market for the products of social labour (that then become commodities), capital and labour. Within its area of operation it brings a tendency to uniformity in the price of identical commodities and returns on capital and labour (in the form of wages or returns to the petty commodity producer). This is a close approximation to the empirical reality in central capitalist formations. But on the scale of the world capitalist system, the worldwide law of value operates on the basis of a truncated market that integrates trade in goods and the movement of capital but excludes the labour force. The worldwide law of value tends to make the cost of commodities uniform but not the rewards for labour. The discrepancies in world pay rates are considerably broader than in productivities. It follows from this thesis that the polarising effect of the worldwide law of value has nothing in common in terms of its quality, quantity and planetary scope with the limited tendencies to polarisation within the former (regional) tributary systems.

In this context the qualitative break represented by capitalism remains totally valid; it manifests itself in a fundamental reversal: the dominance of the economic replaces that of the political and ideological. That is why the world capitalist system is qualitatively different from all previous systems. The latter were of necessity regional, no matter how intensive the relations they were able to maintain among each other. Until the reversal has occurred it is impossible to speak of anything but protocapitalist elements,

15

where they exist, subject to the prevailing tributary logic. That is why I am not convinced of the usefulness of a theoretical view that suppresses this qualitative break and sees a supposedly eternal world system in a continuum whose origin is lost in the distant past of history.

The significance of the qualitative break of capitalism cannot, therefore, be underestimated. But an acknowledgement of it reveals its limited historical application, as it is stripped of the sacred vestments in which bourgeois ideology has dressed it. The simple and reassuring equations can no longer be written, such as capitalism (nowadays market) equals freedom and democracy, etc. For my part, along with Karl Polanyi, I give a central place to the Marxist theory of economic alienation. With Polanyi, I draw the conclusion that capitalism is by its nature synonymous not with freedom, but with oppression. The socialist ideal of bringing freedom from alienation is thus reinvested with all the force of which some sought to deprive it.

The critique of Eurocentrism in no way implies refusal to recognise the qualitative break capitalism represents and, to use a word no longer fashionable, the progress (albeit relative and historically limited progress) it ushers in. Nor does it propose an act of contrition by which westerners renounce describing this invention as European. The critique is of another kind and centred on the contradictions the capitalist era opens up. The system conquers the world but does not make it homogenous. Quite the reverse, it effects the most phenomenal polarisation possible. If the requirement of universalism the system ushers in is renounced, the system cannot be superseded. To sum up in a phrase, the critique I suggested in *Eurocentrism*: the truncated universalism of capitalist economism, necessarily Eurocentric, must be replaced by the authentic universalism of a necessary and possible socialism. In other words, the critique of Eurocentrism must not be backward-looking, making 'a virtue of the difference' as the saying goes.

The mercantalist transition in Europe, 1500-1800

The world system is not reducible to the relatively recent form of capitalism dating back only to the final third of the 19th century, with the onset of imperialism (in the sense that Lenin attached to this term) and the accompanying colonial division of the world. On the contrary, we say that this world dimension of capitalism found expression right from the outset and remained a constant of the system through the successive phases of its development. The recognition that the essential elements of capitalism crystallised in Europe during the Renaissance suggests 1492 – the beginning of the conquest of America – as the date of the simultaneous birth of both capitalism and the world capitalist system, the two phenomena being inseparable.

How should we qualify the nature of the transition from 1500 to 1800? Various qualifications have been suggested, based on the political norms prevailing at the time (Ancien Régime or the Age of Absolute Monarchy) or character of its economy (mercantilism). Indeed, the old mercantilist societies of Europe and the Atlantic and their extension towards central and eastern Europe are problematic. Let us simply note that these societies witnessed the conjunction of certain key preliminary elements of the crystallisation of the capitalist mode of production. These key elements are a marked extension of the field of commodity exchanges affecting a high proportion of agricultural production; an affirmation of modern forms of private ownership and the protection of these forms by the law; a marked extension of free wage labour (in agriculture and craftsmanship). However, the economy of these societies was more mercantile (dominated by trade and exchange) than capitalist by virtue of the fact that the development of the forces of production had not yet imposed the factory as the principal form of production.

As this is a fairly obvious case of a transitional form, I shall make two further comments on this conclusion. First, the elements in question – that some have called protocapitalist (and why not?) – did not miraculously emerge in 1492. They can be found long before in the region, in the Mediterranean precinct particularly, in the Italian cities and across the sea in the Arab-

Islamic world. They had also existed for a very long time in other regions: in India, China, etc. Why then begin the transition to capitalism in 1492 and not in 1350, or in 900, or even earlier? Why speak of transition to capitalism only for Europe and not also describe as societies in transition toward capitalism the Arab-Islamic or Chinese societies in which these elements of proto-capitalism can be found? Indeed, why not abandon the notion of transition altogether, in favour of a constant evolution of a system in existence for a long while, in which the elements of proto-capitalism have been present since very ancient times? My second comment explains in part my hesitation in following the suggestions made above. The colonisation of America accelerated to an exceptional extent the expansion of the protocapitalist elements indicated above. For three centuries the social system that participated in the colonisation were dominated by such elements. This had not been the case elsewhere or before. On the contrary, the protocapitalist segments of society had remained cloistered in a world dominated by tributary social relations (feudal in medieval Europe). So let us now clarify what we mean here by the domination of tributary relations.

One question we might ask is whether the dense network of Italian cities did or did not constitute a protocapitalist system. Undoubtedly protocapitalist forms were present at the level of the social and political organisation of these dominant cities. But can the Italian cities (and even others, in south Germany, the Hanseatic cities, etc) really be separated from the wider body of medieval Christendom? That wider body remained dominated by feudal rural life, with its ramifications at the political and ideological level: customary law, the fragmentation of powers, cultural monopoly of the church, and so on. In this spirit it seems to me essential to give due weight to the evolution of the political system of protocapitalist Europe from the 16th to the 18th century. The evolution that led from the feudal fragmentation of medieval power to the centralisation of the absolute monarchy kept pace precisely with the acceleration of protocapitalist developments. This European specificity is remarkable, since elsewhere – in China or in the Arab-Islamic world for example – there is no known equivalent of feudal fragmentation: the (centralised) state precedes peripheral character of the feudal society – the product of a grafting of the Mediterranean tributary formation onto a body still largely at the backward communal stage (the Europe of the Barbarians).

The (belated) crystallisation of the state, in the form of absolute monarchy, implied, at the outset, relations between the state and the various components of the society that differed abstractly from those that were the case for the central tributary state. The central tributary state merged with the tributary dominant class, which had no existence outside it. The state of the European absolute monarchies was, on the contrary, built on the ruins of the power of the tributary class of the peripheral modality and relied strongly in its state-building on the protocapitalist urban elements (the nascent bourgeoisie) and rural elements (peasantry evolving towards the market). Absolutism resulted form this balance between the new and rising protocapitalist forces and the vestiges of feudal exploitation.

An echo of this specificity can be found in the ideology accompanying the formation of the state of the Ancien Régime, from the Renaissance to the Enlightenment of the 18th century. I stress the specificity – and in my opinion advanced character – of this ideology, which broke with the tributary ideology. In the latter scheme, the predominance of metaphysical view of the world is based on the dominance of the political instance over the economic base. To avoid any misunderstanding, I stress that metaphysics is not synonymous with irrationality (as the radical currents of the Enlightenment have painted it), but seeks to reconcile Reason and Faith (see my discussion of this theme in *Eurocentrism*). The ideological revolution from the Renaissance to the Enlightenment did not suppress metaphysics (metaphysical needs), but freed the sciences from their subjection to it and thereby paved the way to the constitution of a new scientific field, that of the social sciences. At the same time, of course, (far from accidental) concomitance between the practices of the new state (of the Ancien Régime) and developments in the field of ideology began to move rapidly towards the bourgeois revolution (1688 in England, 1776 in New England, 1789 in France). They challenged the absolutist system that had provided a platform for protocapitalist advances. New concepts of power legitimised by democracy (however qualified) were introduced. It is also from there on that the Europeans developed a new awareness of their specificity. Before the Renaissance, the Europeans (of medieval Christendom) knew they were not superior (in power potential) to the advanced societies of the Orient, even if they regarded their religion as superior, just as the others did! From the Renaissance on, they knew they had acquired at least potential superiority over all the other societies and could henceforth conquer the entire globe, which they proceeded to do.

The Arab-Islamic and the Mediterranean prior systems

Everybody knows that the Arab-Islamic Mediterranean and Middle East region enjoyed a brilliant civilisation even before the Italian cities. But did the Arab-Islamic world constitute protocapitalist systems? The protocapitalist forms are present and, at certain times and places, inspired a glorious civilisation. The views I have put forward on this subject (see *The Arab Nation, Eurocentrism*) tie in with Mansour Fawzy's book (1990) on the historical roots of the impasse of the Arab world and, in some regards, with the works of the late Ahmad Sadek Saad. Beyond possible divergences – or shades of meaning – we are of the common opinion that the Arab-Islamic political system was not dominated by protocapitalist (mercantilist) forces but, on the contrary, that the protocapitalist elements remained subject to the logic of the dominant tributary system power. In fact, I consider the Arab-Islamic world as part of a larger regional system, which I call the Mediterranean system.

I have suggested (in *Eurocentrism*) that we can date the birth of this Mediterranean system from the conquests of Alexander the Great (3rd century BC) and conceptualise a single long historic period from this date to the Renaissance, encompassing at first the 'Ancient Orient' (around the eastern basin of the Mediterranean), then the Mediterranean as whole and its Arab-Islamic and European extensions.

I have in this regard put forward the thesis that we are dealing with a single tributary system from 300 BC (unification of the Orient by Alexander the Great) to 1492. I refer to a single 'cultural area' whose unity is manifested in a common metaphysical formulation (the Tributary ideology of the region), beyond the successive expressions of this metaphysics (Hellenistic, Eastern Christian, Islamic, Western Christian). In this tributary area I find it useful to distinguish between its central regions (the Mediterranean Orient) and its peripheral regions (the European West). Within this entity exchanges of every kind have (nearly always) been highly intensive and the associated protocapitalist forms highly advanced, particularly evident in the central regions (in the period of the first flowering of Islam from the 8th to the 12th centuries and in Italy for the succeeding centuries). These exchanges have been the means of a significant redistribution of surplus. However, the eventual centralisation of surplus was essentially tried to the centralisation of political power. From that point of view the cultural area as a whole never constituted a single unified imperial state (except for the two brief periods of the Alexandrine empire and the Roman empire occupying all the central regions of the system). Generally speaking, the peripheral region of the European West remained extremely fragmented under the feudal form (and this is the very expression of its peripheral character). The central region was divided between the Christian Byzantine Orient and the Arab-Islamic empires (the Umayyad, then the Abbasid dynasties). It was first subject to internal centrifugal forces, then belatedly unified in the Ottoman empire, whose establishment coincided with the end of the period and the overall peripheralisation of the eastern region – to the benefit of a shift of the centre towards the previously peripheral region of Europe and the Atlantic.

Could this system be described as protocapitalist? In support of the thesis is the presence of undeniable protocapitalist elements (private ownership, commodity enterprise, wage labour) throughout the period, expanding in certain places and times (especially in the Islamic area and in Italy), declining in others (especially in barbarian Europe of the first millennium). But in my view the presence of these elements does not suffice to characterise the system. On the contrary, I would argue that, at the crucial level of ideology, what began in the Hellenistic phase of this period (from 300 BC to the first centuries AD), and then flourished in the (Eastern then Western) Christian and Islamic forms, is purely and simply the tributary ideology, with its major fundamental characteristic: the predominance of metaphysical concerns.

What we are talking about is indeed a system, but not a proto-capitalist system, that is, a stage in the rapid transition form tributary society to capitalist society. On the other hand, we are dealing with a tributary system, not a mere juxtaposition of autonomous tributary societies (in the plural), which just happened to share some common elements, such as religion, for example, or integration – albeit of limited duration – in an imperial state, such as that of Rome, Byzantium, the Umayyad or Abbasid dynasties.

The distinction implies in my view a certain degree of centralisation of surplus, which took the form of tribute and not, as in capitalism, that of profit from capital. The normal method of centralisation of this tributary surplus was political centralisation, operating to the advantage of imperial capitals (Rome, Byzantium, Damascus, Baghdad). Of course this centralisation remained weak, as did the authority of the centres concerned. Byzantium, Damascus, and Baghdad could not prevent their staging-posts (Alexandria, Cairo, Fez, Kairouan, Genoa, Venice, Pisa, and so on) from frequently achieving their own autonomy. The entirety of barbican Christendom (the first millennium in the West) escaped such centralisation. In parallel, the logic of the centralisation of authority stimulated protocapitalist relations to the point that mercantile handling of part of the surplus never disappeared from the region, and took on great significance in some areas and epochs, notably during the glorious centuries of Islam, and the emergence of the Italian cities following the Crusades. On this basis I have described the social formations of the Arab world as tributary-mercantile formations. All this leads me to conclude that capitalism might have been born in the Arab world. This takes me back to other discussions on this issue with which I have been associated. I have argued that once capitalism had appeared in Europe and the Atlantic, the process of evolution towards capitalism was brutally halted in its development elsewhere. The reason why the evolution towards capitalism accelerated in the Atlantic West (shifting the centre of gravity of the system from the banks of the Mediterranean to the shores of the Atlantic ocean), it seems to me, is mainly due to the colonisation (of America, then of the entire globe) and contingently to the peripheral character of Western feudalism.

Did a single world tributary system exist?

My methodological hypothesis leads me to regard the other cultural areas as further autonomous tributary systems. In particular, it seems to me that the Confucian-Chinese tributary system constituted a world on its own and of its own. It had its own centre (China), characterised by a strong political centralisation (even if the latter under the pressure of internal centrifugal forces exploded from time to time, it was always reconstituted), and its peripheries (Japan especially) had a relationship with China very similar to that of medieval Europe with the civilised Orient. I leave a dotted line after the question of whether the Hindu cultural area constituted a (single) tributary system.

This having been said, the question is: was the Mediterranean system isolated or in close relation with the other Asiatic and African systems? Can the existence of a permanent world system, in constant evolution, be argued beyond the Mediterranean area and prior to its constitution? A positive response to this question has been suggested to some (notably Frank) by the intensity of exchange relations between the protocapitalist Mediterranean, the Chinese and Indian Orient, and sub-Saharan Africa, and perhaps even the significance of the exchanges in earlier times between these various regions of the ancient world. For my part, I do not believe that it is possible to answer the questions, given the current state of knowledge. It is, however, useful to raise it in order to provoke a systematic exchange of views on what can be deduced from our knowledge, the hypotheses it may inspire, and the directions of research indicated for verification of these hypotheses.

I do not intend to substitute my own 'intuitive views' for the eventual results of these debates. I advance them here only provisionally, to open the discussion. I should therefore suggest the following (provisional) theses.

First, humankind is one since its origins. The itinerary of the earth's population begins from the nucleus of hominids appearing in East Africa, going down the Nile and populating Africa, crossing the Mediterranean and the Isthmus of Suez to conquer Europe and Asia, passing the Bering Straits and perhaps crossing the Pacific to install themselves (in the most recent epoch) in the

Americas. These successive conquests of the planet's territory are beginning to be dated. The following may be the pertinent question: has the dispersal brought a diversification of the lines of evolution of the various human groups, installed in geographical environments of extreme diversity and hence exposed to challenges of differing kinds? Or does the existence of parallel lines of evolution suggest the conclusion that humankind as a whole has remained governed by laws of evolution of universal application? And as a complement to this question, it might be asked what effect have relations between the scattered human populations had on the fate, intensity and rapidity of the transfer of knowledge, experience and ideas?

Intuitively it might be imagined that some human groups have found themselves fairly isolated in particularly difficult circumstances and have responded to the challenge by particular adaptation unlikely to evolve of themselves. These groups would then be located in 'impasses', constrained to reproduce their own organisation without the latter showing signs of its own suppression. Perhaps included here would be the (still highly fragmented) societies of hunters/fishers/gatherers of the Arctic, the equatorial forest, small islands and some coasts.

But other groups have found themselves in less arduous circumstances that have enabled them to progress simultaneously in mastery of nature (passage to settled agriculture, invention of more efficient tools and so on) and in tighter social organisation. In regard to the latter the question arises of possible laws of social evolution of universal application and the role of external relations in this evolution.

Second, in regard to societies that have clearly advanced, can one detect similar phasing followed by all, albeit at faster or slower rates? Our entire social science is based on this seemingly necessary hypothesis. For the satisfaction of the spirit? As legitimation of a universalist value system? Various formulations of this necessary evolution succeeded one another up to and during the 19th century. They were based either on the succession of modes of exploitation of the soil and instruments utilised (Old Stone Age, New Stone Age, Iron Age), or on the succession of social forms of organisation (the ages of Savagery, Barbarism, Civilisation). Various evolutions in these particular domains were regrafted on to what we regarded as fundamental general tendencies. For example, the matriarchal–patriarchal succession, the succession of the ages of philosophical thought (primitive, animist, metaphysical, Auguste Comte-style positivist), and so on. I shall not spend time here discussing these theories, which are almost always more or less overridden by subsequent research. I merely point to their existence as evidence of the persistence of the need to generalise, beyond the evident diversity that is the property of the scientific approach.

It seems to me that the most sophisticated formulation of all the theories of general evolution was that proposed by Marxism and based on the synthetic notions of modes of production. The latter comes from a conceptualisation of the basic elements of the construction (forces of production, relations of production, infrastructure and superstructure, etc). They are then enriched by the grafting on of particular theories articulated to those of modes of production (such as theory of the family, of the state, etc). Here again I shall not discuss whether these Marxist constructs are indeed those of Marx himself, or the product of later interpretations that may or may not be consonant with the spirit of the Marxism of Marx. Nor shall I discuss the validity of these theories in the light of our present-day greater knowledge of the societies of the past. Once again I merely point to the formulations as the expression of this same need to understand, which implies the possibility of generalising.

Third, on the basis of the conceptualisation proposed, it is not difficult to identify several tributary societies at more or less the same level of maturity of general development: production techniques, instruments, range of goods, forms of organisation of power, systems of knowledge and ideas, and so on. Noteworthy too is a fairly dense web of exchanges of all kinds between these societies: exchange of goods, knowledge, techniques, and ideas. Does this density of exchange justify speaking of a single world system (albeit described as tributary) in the singular? Frank provides an explicit criterion: an integrated system arises when reciprocal influences are decisive (A would not be what it is without the relation it has with B). So be it. But the overall question remains: were these relations decisive or not?

However, the universality of the laws of social evolution in no way implies the concept of a single system. Two distinct concepts are involved. The first refers to the fact that distinct societies – separated in geographical distance or time – have been able to evolve in a parallel manner for the same underlying reasons. The second implies that these societies are not distinct from one another but ingredients of the same world society. In the evolution of the latter – necessarily global – the laws in question are inseparable from the effects of the interaction between the various components of the world society.

I would in this context make two prefatory comments. First, economic exchanges are not necessarily a decorative element, making no lasting impression on the mode of production and hence on the level of development. Exchanges may be a significant means of distribution of surplus, decisive for some segments of the inter-related societies. The question is not one of principle but of fact. Were they? Where and when? I discount any hasty generalisation that they were always (or generally) so or that they were never (or with rare exceptions) so. In the case of the Arab-Islamic region, for example, I have said that the exchanges were significant. They were enough to mark the formation of a tributary–mercantile character essential to an understanding of its involuted history of succession from a 'glorious' phase to one of 'degeneration', and of shifts of the centres of gravity of wealth and power in the region. I have also said that the protocapitalist formation of mercantilist Europe (17th–18th centuries) rapidly climbed the step towards capitalism thanks to these exchanges it dominated. But whether the exchanges had a matching role in China, India, the Roman empire, etc, I personally am in no position to say. Second, the exchanges in question must not be limited only to the economic field; far from it. The writing of the history of the precapitalist epochs puts greater emphasis on cultural exchanges (especially the spread of religions) and military and political exchanges (rise and fall of empires, 'barbarian' invasions, etc), whereas the accent is on the economic aspect of relations within the modern world system. Was this distinction wrong?

I do not think so. I believe, on the contrary, that the historians – albeit intuitively – have grasped the reversal of dominance, from the political and ideological to the economic, which is the central core of my own thesis. At this level is it possible to speak of a single tributary political and ideological world system? I do not believe so. I have therefore preferred to speak of distinct tributary 'cultural areas' founded precisely on broad systems of particular reference – most often the religious: Confucianism, Hinduism, Islam, Christianity. Of course there is a certain relationship between these various metaphysics since they express the fundamental requirement of the same type of (tributary) society. The relationship in turn facilitates mutual borrowings. To approach an answer to the question (of one or more systems), it is necessary to combine three elements: the density of economic exchanges and transfers of surplus distributed through this channel; the degree of centralisation of political power; and the relative diversity/specificity and hence autonomy of the ideological systems. Autonomy of the various tributary systems does not preclude economic relations and other exchanges among them, nor even that such exchanges could be significant. It would be impossible to understand many historical facts and evolutions without reference to these exchanges: the transfer of technology of all kinds (the compass, gunpowder, paper, silk that gave its name to the roads in question, printing, Chinese noodles becoming Italian pasta, etc); the spread of religious beliefs (Buddhism crossing from India to China and Japan, Islam travelling as far as Indonesia and China, Christianity as far as Ethiopia, south India, and central Asia), etc.

There is certainly no centralisation of surplus at the level of a world system comparable to that characterising the modern world in the exchanges that led here and there to lively protocapitalist links (from China and India to the Islamic world, the African Sahel and medieval Europe) and transfers of surplus – perhaps even decisive at key points of the network of exchanges. The explanation is that centralisation of surplus at the time operated mainly in association with the centralisation of power, and there was no kind of world empire or even a world power comparable to what British hegemony would constitute in the 19th century or United States hegemony in the 20th. The ancient (tributary) epochs had nothing comparable to the polarisation on a global scale of the modern capitalist world. The earlier systems, despite significant levels of exchange, were not polarising on a world scale, even if they were on a regional scale to the benefit of the centres of the regional systems (for example, Rome, Constantinople, Baghdad, the Italian cities, China, India). By contrast, the capitalist system is truly polarising on a global scale and is therefore the only one deservedly described as a world system. This methodology for the analysis of the interactions between the tributary systems may call for a reassessment of the traditional findings in the history of the notorious 'barbarians' who occupied the interstices of the great tributary cultural areas. Was the role of these barbarians really as it has been made out, a purely negative and destructive role? Or did their active role in inter-tributary exchanges give them a certain vocation to take decisive initiatives? The latter would explain their success (not only military) in unifying immense territories (Genghis Khan's empire), their capacity to situate themselves at the heart of ideological initiatives (Islam born in Arabia, the barbarian crossroads of Mediterranean–Indian–African exchanges), their capacity to hoist themselves rapidly to central positions in a tributary system (the glorious example of the Khwarizm area in the first centuries of Islam), etc.

A final reservation concerning the systematisation of the hypothesis of the existence of a single world system throughout history: is it possible to speak of tributary systems and significant exchange networks among them before the 5th to 3rd centuries BC? I do not think so for the following three reasons at least: (1) because the social systems of the greater part of humankind were still backward at the stage I have described as communal; (2) because the islets of civilisation at the stage where the state was the recognised form of the expression of power had not yet found complete tributary ideological expression (see the argument on the ideology of the ancient world in *Eurocentrism*); (3) because the density of the exchange relations between these islets remained weak (this did not preclude some exchange relations; for example, technological borrowings that were able to travel unexpected distances).

A critique of evolutionism

The theory according to which all human societies have been for-ever integrated in a single world system, in continuous evolution (capitalism not representing, therefore, any kind of qualitative break in this respect) arises from a philosophy of history which is in the end based on the notion of competition. Certainly it is based on a realistic observation of facts, namely, that all societies on earth, in all eras, are to some extent in competition with one another – it would not matter whether the relations they did or did not entertain showed their awareness of it. We know that the strongest must carry the day. At this level of abstraction there is indeed a single world, because there is a single humankind. It might perhaps be added that most 'open' societies with intensive relations with the others have a greater chance of measuring up to this competition and facing up to it more effectively. It is otherwise for those who shy away from competition and seek to perpetuate their way of life; they risk being overtaken by the progress made elsewhere and later being marginalised.

This discourse is not wrong, but merely at such a high level of abstraction that it begs the real issue, namely, how this competition is manifested. Two bourgeois historians – themselves philosophers of history – deliberately placed themselves at this most general level of abstraction (in order to refute Marx). Arnold Toynbee in this regard suggests an operative model reduced to two terms: the challenge and the response to the challenge. I suggest that as a model valid for all times and all places, it teaches us nothing that is not already obvious. Toynbee suggests no law to explain why the challenge is taken up or not. He is satisfied with a case-by-case treatment. There is an almost natural parallel with the contradiction between the axioms of neoclassical bourgeois economics defined in terms claiming to be valid for all times (scarcity, utility, etc) and the historical concept of qualitatively differing successive modes of production, determining specific institutional frameworks in which the 'eternal rationality of human beings' is expressed. Jacques Pirenne, far superior to Toynbee in my opinion, suggests a refinement of constant contradiction between (sea-going) open societies and (land-based) closed societies and does not hesitate to describe the former as capitalist (Sumer, Phoenicia, Greece, Islam in the first centuries, the Italian cities, the modern West) and the latter as feudal (from ancient Persia to the European Middle Ages). He never hesitated to attribute to what I call proto-capitalist elements the decisive place in the progress of the open societies making the driving force of development of the forces of production. He likewise never concealed that his thesis was

29

intended to discount the closed experiences of the Soviet Union and salute the dynamism of the Atlantic world. Hence, Pirenne managed – certainly with skill – to replace class struggle with a constant struggle between the capitalist tendency and the feudal tendency within human societies.

I still believe that Marx's method is superior, precisely because it situates the abstraction at the appropriate level. The concept of modes of production gives back to history its explicit real dimension. At that level the significance and character of the capitalist break can be detected. The break is such that I do not think that competition between societies of earlier times and within the modern world system can be treated in the same way. First, because the competition of earlier times rarely crossed the threshold of consciousness and each society saw, or believed, itself 'superior' in its own way, protected by its deities, even when a looming danger imposed a greater consciousness (as between Muslims and Crusaders). Moreover, the discrepancy between the great tributary pre-capitalist societies is not such that the superiority of one over another is obvious; it is always conjunctural and relative. There is nothing comparable to the subsequent overwhelming superiority of capitalist societies over the rest. That is why I see the seizing of consciousness of this superiority as crucially important and therefore date the beginnings of capitalism to 1492. From then on the Europeans knew that they could conquer the world and went on to do so (see my arguments on this point in *Eurocentrism*). We know, *a posteriori* (but the actors of the time were unaware), that the 'strongest' is the one who has advanced to a qualitatively superior mode of production – capitalism. I would add that in the competition of earlier times geographical distance had a blunting effect. However intensive the exchanges between Rome and China, I find it difficult to believe that the external factor could have a similar impact to that of the discrepancies in productivity of our own times. I believe that this distancing gave strictly internal factors a considerably more decisive relative weight. It also explains why those concerned had difficulty in assessing the real balance of forces. Quite different, it seems to me, is competition within the modern world system, where consciousness is so acute that it is a plaintive chorus in the daily discourse of the authorities.

1 ANCIENT WORLD SYSTEMS VS CAPITALIST WORLD SYSTEM

A diagram of the tributary regional and world systems

Figure 1 illustrates my concept of the ancient world system (reduced to societies of the so-called eastern hemisphere: Eurasia–Africa) for the periods covering the eighteen centuries between the establishment of the Hellenistic system in the Middle East (300 BC), the establishment of the Han state in China (200 BC), the Kushāna and Maurya states in Central Asia and India (200 BC), and the European Renaissance, that is, from 300 BC to 1500 AD. I wish to summarise its characteristics as follows.

First, as I have already said, all societies of the system in question are, from one end of the period to the other, of a tributary nature. Nevertheless, it is possible to distinguish among all these societies those which I would call central tributaries from those which are peripheral tributaries. The former are characterised by a surplus centralisation at the relatively high state level, with its redistribution placed under its control; while in peripheral formations, the embryonic character of the state (and even its virtual non-existence) leads to a complete disintegration of surplus distribution monopolised by local feudal systems. The centres/peripheries antithesis is not, in this case, analogous to that which characterises the (modern) capitalist world. In the latter, the relationship in question is an economic domination relationship in which the centres override the peripheries (and this is associated with economic dominance). This is not so in the ancient relationship. Dominated by the ideological authority, the tributary structures are either central or peripheral depending on the degree of the completion of the power centralisation process and its expression through a state religion. In the central formations, the latter takes the form of a state religion or a religious-oriented state philosophy with a universal vocation which breaks with the specific local religions of the former periods which I called 'communal formations' (see *Class and Nation*). There is a striking relationship between the establishment of big tributary societies in their completed form and the emergence of great religious and philosophical trends which were to dominate civilisations over the ensuing 2,000 years: Hellenism (300 BC), Oriental Christianity, Islam (600 AD), Zoroaster, Buddha, and Confucius (all three 500 BC).

This relationship – which in no way excluded the reciprocal concessions provided by the relations that all tributary civilisations maintained among themselves – is not, in my view, an accident, but rather one of the consistent bases of my thesis on the dominant tributary mode.

The establishment of great philosophical and religious movements associated with the formation of tributary systems represents the first wave of revolutions related to universal history, which is expressed by a universalist-oriented vocation transcending the horizons of the local – almost parochial – line of thinking in the ancient periods. This revolution sets up the tributary system as a general system at the entire level of mankind – or almost does so – for 2,000 to 2,500 years. The second wave of universal-oriented revolutions, which opens up capitalist modernity and its possible socialist overtaking, is marked by the Renaissance (and the revolution in Christianity with which it is associated) and, subsequently, by the three great modern revolutions: the French, Russian and Chinese revolutions (see *Eurocentrism*).

The model *par excellence* of this tributary mode is, in my view, provided by China which, without it seems a long incubation period (there is only one millennium between the Shang and the Zhu and the establishment of the Han dynasty), crystallises in a form which undergoes no fundamental change, either with regard to the organisation of productive forces and production relationships or ideology (the Confucianism–Taoism tandem replaced for only a brief moment by Buddhism), or with regard to power concepts during the 2,000 years between the Han dynasty and the 1911 revolution. Here, surplus centralisation is at its height, at the level of an enormous society, not only during the brilliant periods where political unity was entirely or almost entirely achieved in this continent-country by great successive dynasties (Han, Tāng, Sōng, Yuán, Ming and Qing), but even during the periods of interdynastic disturbances when the country was divided into several kingdoms whose size was nonetheless considerable for the period. At the borders of China, Korea and Vietnam also turned, during the course of the first millennium of our era, into similar tributary systems which, in spite of their political independence with regard to China, borrowed its model of organisation and Confucian ideology.

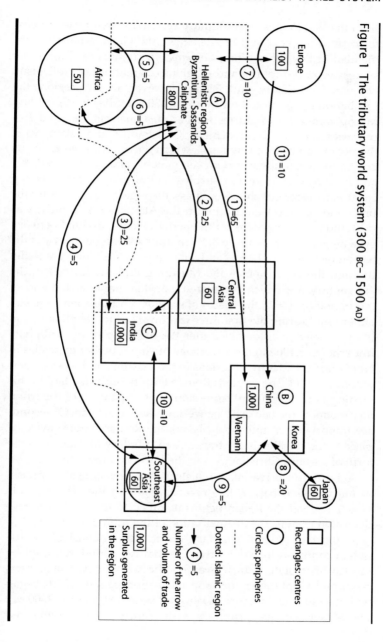

Figure 1 The tributary world system (300 BC–1500 AD)

In the Middle East, the tributary system derived its completed form from the conquest of Alexander the Great. I have recommended in this connection (see *Eurocentrism*) this reading of the successive philosophical and religious orientations of Hellenism, Oriental Christianity, and Islam. However, in this region, the incubation period lasted for as long as 30 centuries for Egypt and Mesopotamia, ten centuries for Persia, Phoenicia, etc, and five centuries for Greece. Hellenism, Christianity, and Islam were, moreover, to produce a synopsis which borrowed some elements crucial to each of these ancient components and even from Persia and India as well. Here, too, surplus centralisation for the ensuing 2,000 years is remarkable. Doubtless, the region was split after the precarious political unification in the Alexander era; but it was split into large kingdoms for the period. Hence, divided between even bigger empires – those of Byzantium (300 to 1400 AD) and the Sassanids (200 to 600 AD) – and subsequently reunified gradually through the expansion of the Muslim Caliphate, formed in the 7th century AD, which conquered Constantinople at the end of our period (in 1453), the spaces of surplus centralisation were still either vast (during the first three centuries of the Caliphate), or at the very least, considerable, after the break-up of the Caliphate from the year 1000 to the advantage of Arabo-Berber dynasties in North Africa and Turco-Persians in the Mashreq and western part of Central Asia. The western Roman empire finds its place in this reading of history as an expression of an expansion of the tributary model to the banks of the western Mediterranean. Of secondary importance in universal history, the Roman empire owes its place to the fact that it has transmitted tributary ideology – in the form of western Christianity – to the European periphery.

A Eurocentric reading of history (see my critical appraisal in *Eurocentrism*) has, in this regard, distorted the achievements which, beyond the Italian peninsula failed to resist barbaric feudalisation (that is, the disintegration of the tributary system).

A third completed tributary centre was established on the Indian continent in 200 BC from the Maurya period, followed by the Kushāna state (which overlaps the western part of Central Asia) and Gupta after the long incubation period which began with the Indus civilisations (Mohenjodaro and Harappa – 2500 BC). The Muslim conquest from the 11th century on which followed after a 'pulverisation' period (of the 7th and 9th centuries) re-established together with the Ghazhavids, the Sultanates of Delhi (1200–1500 AD), and subsequently the Mughal empire (1500–1800 AD), a tributary centralisation on a large scale, while the Hinduist states of Dekkan, also tributaries, equally represented consider-able kingdoms for the period.

Three zones are shown in Figure 1 whose peripheral character is striking during the entire or almost entire period under consid-eration (from 300 BC to 1500 AD). Europe (beyond the Byzantine region and Italian, that is, 'barbaric' Europe), was the product of a tributary graft (transmitted by the ideal of the Roman empire and Christian universalism) on a social body still organised, to a large extent, on deteriorated community bases. Here, I wish to refer to the analysis I made (see *Class and Nation*) which simultaneously gives an account of the disintegration in the control of surpluses, and which defines feudalism as an uncompleted peripheral form of the tributary system, although the collapse of the state system was partially offset by the church. Europe was slowly moving toward the tributary form, as testified by the establishment of absolute monarchies (in Spain and Portugal after the Reconquista, and in England and France after the Hundred Years War). This belatedness constitutes, in my view, the crucial advantage which facilitated the early qualitative strides made by the Renaissance and capitalism (see *Class and Nation*).

Japan constituted, at the other end of the Euro-Asian continent, a peripheral tributary mode whose resemblance to Europe had struck me even before Mishio Morishima came to confirm my thesis. The degraded form of Japanese Confucianism, the feudal disintegration which preceded the belated formation of a monar-chical centralisation from the Tokugawa State (1600 AD) bear testi-mony to this peripheral character (see *Eurocentrism*), which, here, too, explains the remarkable ease with which Japan switched over to capitalism in the 19th century. Sub-Saharan Africa constituted the third periphery. It was still lingering at the communal stage developing towards tributary forms. At this stage the tributary surplus centralisations still operated only on societies with lim-ited size. Disintegration therefore remained the rule.

The status of Southeast Asia was ambivalent. It seems to me that here it is possible to recognise some central type of tributary formations – even if they only cover smaller spaces than those of other great Asian systems – and peripheral zones (defined by surplus disintegration). To the first type belongs the Khmer empire, followed by its Thai, Burmese and Cambodian successors from the 5th century and, perhaps, in Indonesia, the Majapahit kingdom from the 13th century. On the other hand, the organised societies of Malaysia and Indonesia which crystallised into states under the influence of Hinduism (from the 5th century) and subsequently Islam, seem, in my view, to belong to the peripheral family, crumbled by the scattering of the surplus, collected in very small and relatively numerous and fragile states. The status of the Central Asian region was special. The region itself is less defined in its borders than the others. Some large states were established in this region at an early period – such as the Kushāna empire – which directly linked up the Hellenistic Middle East and the Sassanids and then the Islamic Middle East to India and China. The region itself became the centre of gravity of an immense empire at the time of Genghis Khan (1300 AD). Before and after this final crystallisation, it had entered the Islamic orbit. Its modes of organisation were tributary-oriented, at one time advanced (where the expression of centralised power on a large scale makes it possible), at another time relapsing into feudal disintegration. But the major feature of the region was that, by virtue of its very geographical position, it was the indispensable transit zone for East–West trade (China, India, the Middle East and beyond to as far as the peripheries of the system). Having been in competition with the sea route from time immemorial, the continental route lost its importance only belatedly in the 16th century.

As for the second characteristic of the ancient world system: during the entire 18th-century period under consideration, all the societies represented in Figure 1 not only existed together, but still maintained trade links of all types (trade and war, technological and cultural transfers), which were much more intense than was generally thought. In this very general sense, one can talk of the general system without, of course, mistaking its nature for that of the modern (capitalist) world system. In Figure 1, I represent these links by eleven arrows. Of course, the intensity of flows that each of these arrows represents varied considerably with time and space. But above all – and I wish to emphasise this point – their connection with the internal dynamics peculiar to the different tributary systems they link up is not only fundamentally different from that which characterises the international links within the modern world system, but has also operated differently from one tributary formation to another. To clarify things, I want to distinguish four sets of links:

1. The links mutually maintained between the three major centres (A – Rome and Byzantium, the Sassanid empire, the Caliphate; B – China; C – India) are marked by arrows 1 (Middle East–China through central and Northern Asia), 2 (Middle East–India across western central Asia), and 3 (Middle East–India by sea route). These links were undoubtedly the most intense of all, merely in view of the wealth and relative power of the centres in question, at least in the glorious years of their history.

2. The links maintained by the Arabo-Persian Islamic centre with the three peripheries (Europe, Africa, Southeast Asia) are shown by arrows 4 (Middle East–Malaysia, Indonesia sea route), 5 (North Africa–African Sahel trans-Saharan route), 6 (Middle East–Swahili eastern coast sea route), and 7 (Caliphate and Byzantium–Europe). The trade in question was less intense than that of the previous group (due to the relative poverty of the peripheries), and especially important is the fact that it was asymmetrical (a concept that I clearly distinguish from the specific inequality of the centres/peripheries relationships of the modern world) in the sense that they were perhaps neutral in their effects on the centre, but crucial for the development of the peripheries. These relationships considerably accelerated the establishment of states in the African Sahel and East Africa (see *Class and Nation*) as well as in Malaysia and Indonesia and thus opened the way for the Islamisation of these regions (Islam then replacing the ancient local religions in line with the needs of the tributary world). They also contributed immensely to the emergence of Italian trading cities and, through these cities, of infiltration throughout the whole of feudal Europe.

3. The links maintained by the Chinese centre with the Japanese periphery (arrow 8) and the Southeast Asian

periphery (arrow 9) are of the same nature as those in the second group. Here, I wish to refer to arrow 11, which indicates a direct communication establishment between China and Europe, using of course the routes of Central Asia but without passing through the canal in the heart of the Islamic Caliphate. This direct relation existed only for a relatively short period, within the framework of the Mongol Pax (the Genghis Khan empire in the 13th century). But it was crucial for subsequent events of history because it made it possible for Europe to resort to China's vast technological accomplishments (gunpowder, printing, the compass, etc); Europe was mature enough to do this and take the qualitative leap from a peripheral tributary (feudal) system to capitalism. Furthermore, shortly thereafter Europe substituted the sea route it dominated for all ancient forms of long-haul transport, thus establishing direct links between itself and each of the other regions of the world (Africa, India, Southeast Asia), 'discovering' and then 'conquering' America at the same time.

4. The links maintained by the Indian centre (Buddhist and Hindu) with its Southeast Asian peripheries (arrow 10) are similar to the China–Japan links.

It obviously appears that the relative intensity of external flows, as compared with the different masses constituted by the regional formations under consideration, varies considerably from one region to another. The three key central regions, A, B and C (Middle East, China, India), represented, in terms of economic weight, a multiple of what constituted each of the other regions. If, therefore, the volume of the surplus identified in each of these key central regions is measured by index 1,000, it could hardly have exceeded index 100 for each of the other regions (Europe, Africa, Japan, Central Asia and Southeast Asia). Moreover, only a part and probably a relatively minor part (10 to 20 per cent perhaps) of this surplus could involve long-distance trade.

The four arrows which concern China (major 1, minors 8 and 9, and transitory 11) could, for instance, represent an index 'value' of about 100 (10 per cent of the surplus produced in China). The three arrows which concern India (majors 2 and 3 and minor

10) probably hardly exceeded index 50 or 70. All historians have observed that the external trade of these two continental masses were marginal as compared with their volume of production.

On the other hand, the weight of external trade seems more pronounced for region A, which is the only region in direct relationship with all the others. To major arrows 1, 2 and 3 representing A's trade with B and C (total index value: 115 in our assumption) is added the region's trade with the peripheries of Europe (arrow 7), Africa (arrows 5 and 6), and Southeast Asia (arrow 4), making a total index value of about 25. In sum then, external trade, in this case, would have represented an index value of 140 (almost 29 per cent of the surplus).

For each of the peripheries too, the contribution of external trade would appear relatively considerable: index 20 for Europe, 10 for Africa, 20 for Southeast Asia and 20 for Japan, that is 20 to 33 per cent of the surplus generated in these regions. Similarly, transit flows through Central Asia (arrows 1, 2 and 11) on the order of index 100, might have accounted for a volume even greater than that of the locally produced surplus.

The index values assigned to both the surplus volumes produced in each region and the trade volumes indicated by each of the arrows are, of course, mere fabrications on my part, created with a view to suggesting some relative orders of magnitude. It is for historians to improve upon them. Failing this (and we have not found any figures in this regard), the figures I have used constitute some orders of magnitude which seem plausible to me and which can be summarised in Table 1.

Table 1 Locally generated external flows

	Surplus		%
	(1)	(2)	(2/1)
Middle East	800	140	18
China	1,000	100	10
India	1,000	60	6
Europe	100	20	20
Africa	50	10	20
Japan	60	20	33
Southeast Asia	60	20	33
Central Asia	60	100	166

Geography has assigned to key central region A an exceptional role without any possible competitor until modern times, when Europe, through its control over the seas, overcame the constraints. Indeed, this region is directly linked to all the others (China, India, Europe, Africa) and is the only one as such. For two millennia, it was an indispensable transit route to Europe, China, India or Africa. Besides, the region does not reflect a relative homogeneity similar to that of China or India, neither at the geographical level (stretching from the Moroccan shores of the Atlantic to the Aral Sea, Pamirs and to the Oman Sea, it does not have the features of a continental block as in the case of China and India), nor at the level of its peoples, who themselves are products of the early proliferation of the most ancient civilisations (Egypt, Sumer, Assyria, Mesopotamia, Iran, Hittites, Phoenicians and Greeks) and speak languages from various families (Semitic, Hamitic, Indo-European). The conquest of Alexander the Great and the triumph of the Hellenistic synthesis triggered a collective awareness which was subsequently strengthened by Oriental Christianity (limited by the Sassanid border) and subsequently and, above all, by Islam.

One of the keys to the success of Islam relates, in my view, to this reality. The region was finally firmly established within the short period covering the first three centuries of the Hegira. It was thus composed of the three superimposed strata of Islamised peoples, namely, the Arabs from the Atlantic to the Gulf, the Persians beyond Zagros to Pakistan, the Turks in Anatolia and in the entire Turkestan from the Caspian Sea to China proper. Thus, Islam did not only unify the peoples of the so-called classical 'East' but annexed, at the same time, Central Asia, the indispensable transit route to China and northern India. I think that this success should be attributed to the fact that in spite of all the conflicts witnessed by history internal to this region, it created a certain solidarity and strengthened the sense of a particular identity with regard to the 'others'; that is, specifically, the Chinese, Indians, Europeans and Africans that the Muslim *umma* borders on along each of its frontiers. In Central Asia the success of Islam created regional unity, which, until then, was absent. For the civilisation in this region, in which trade flows represent larger volumes than the surplus produced locally, depended on the capacity to capture, in passing, a part of these transit flows.

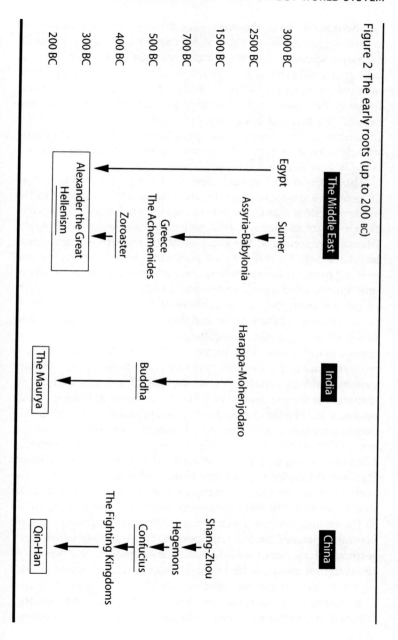

Figure 2 The early roots (up to 200 BC)

The magnitude of the links with the others for the entire key central region A and its Central Asia annex bestows on its social system a special character which I venture, for this reason, to call 'mercantile-tributary', thus indicating even the magnitude of protocapitalist forms (commercial links, wage labour, private property or estate) in the tributary societies of Islam. Moreover, beyond the original boundaries of Islam, the gradual conquest of African and Southeast Asian peripheries is also worth putting into close relationship with its mercantile dynamism of region A (see *The Arab Nation, Class and Nation*).

Third, the world system described above for the period of 18 centuries preceding the Renaissance is not analogous to the modern system that follows it (in time). To talk about the ancient system in its spatial and time universality or even in its Arab–Islamic component as the ancestor of the modern system would be misleading. For this is only a platitude – succession in time and nothing more; or it implies that there was no qualitative break but only quantitative development and a shift of the system's centre of gravity from the southern shore of the Mediterranean to its northern shore (Italian cities) and then to the Atlantic shores, and this boils down to eliminating the essential, that is, the qualitative change in the nature of the system: the law of value which governs the dynamics of the modern system but not those of the tributary system. This universalisation of the law of value is exclusively responsible for the establishment of one single antinomy which operates worldwide (a centre composed of historically established national centres as such and peripheries all economically dependent on this centre), thus creating an *ever-increasing* differentiation from one period to another between the centre and the peripheries, over the entire five-century history of capitalism and for the entirely visible or imaginable horizon within the framework of its immanent laws. In this connection, there is nothing comparable to the lasting relative balance (for 2,000 years!) between the key central regions of the tributary period. This qualitative difference forbids talking about interdependence – unequal, as it were – of the different components of the ancient system in terms similar to those that govern the modern world. Key regions A, B and C are certainly in relation with one another (and with the other regions). It remains to be demonstrated that this interdependence would have been essential. The parallelism in their trend is no evidence of the crucial nature of their relations; it only reflects the general character of the laws governing the social development of all mankind (thus defining the status of the specificities). The possible concomitance of the rise and the specificities of states of the past is far from obvious.

A cursory glance at Figure 3, which describes the parallel history of the three key centres and the other regions, shows that this concomitance is merely a matter of pure chance.

Pirenne had already observed – a view taken up again by A.G. Frank – the concomitance between the fall of the Roman empire and that of the Han dynasty. But the Roman fall was followed by the rise of Byzantium, the Sassanid and the Kushāna state, while the decline of the Hans was followed, right from the year 600 (the height of barbarianism in the West) by the rise of the Tāng and, three centuries earlier, by that of the Guptas, whose fall coincided (also by chance) with the rise of Islam. There are no clues to the identification of the general cycles of the rise and fall. The very term 'fall' is, even in this context, misleading; it is the fall of a form of state organisation in a given region, but, in most cases, as regards the development of productive forces, there is no parallel fall. I am struck rather by the opposite phenomenon, that is, the continuity of these long parallel historical events: from Rome–Byzantium–Sassanids–Islam to the Ottomans and the Safavids, from the Maurya dynasty to that Mughal state, from the Han dynasty to those of Ming and Qing, there were only a few qualitative changes but a great quantitative progress on the same organisation (tributary) bases. This does not exclude the fact that, in examining local developments, it is possible to explain any particular political rise (or fall) which may still be relative – by a special link in which external relations have occasionally played a role. Once again, there is nothing similar to the cycles of the capitalist economy, whose scope is really global as a result of the universalisation of the law of value, the basis of the modern capitalist economy. The crystallisation of new modernity in Europe which was achieved within a short time (from the rise of Italian cities to the Renaissance: three to four centuries) is not the repetition of a general phenomenon under which would be subsumed all together the birth of civilisations (Egypt, Sumer, Harappa, Shang) and the establishment of empires (Achemenid, Alexander, Rome, Byzantium, Sassanid, Umayyad, Abbasid, Ottoman, Safavid, Maurya, Gupta, the Mughal state, Han, Tāng, Sōng, Ming, Qing and the Genghis Khan empire).

I proposed an explanation of this fact (see *Class and Nation*) that the qualitative break is first made within a tributary periphery (Europe) and not in one of its centres (A, B or C) and is then repeated in another periphery (Japan). I based my explanation on the contrast between the flexibility of the peripheries and the rigidity of the centres, that is, while keeping to the logical context of the general nature of the laws of the evolution of societies (the 'uneven development' which is the general form of an identical overall evolution). I consider this explanation more satisfactory than those proposed by the different characteristically Eurocentric conceptions (see *Eurocentrism*). I also think it is more satisfactory than Pirenne's theory, which I have referred to as being based on the permanent contrast between capitalism (the synonym of openness, especially in maritime terms) and feudalism (the synonym of closure, especially in landlocked terms). Like A.G. Frank's (who is close to the extreme), Pirenne's theory is a transformation of the Eurocentric deformation: it attributes the European miracle to the maritime openness of the region, since each of the theories is based on the negation of the specific nature of the capitalist modernity.

Of course the crystallisation of capitalism in Europe has a history (it is not done by magic, in 1493 for instance) and entails specific consequences for the subsequent evolution of the other regions. The rapid development of Italian cities, which of course accounted for such crystallisation, is in turn a result of the tributary mercantile expansion of the Arab-Islamic region. However, it is because it operated within an outlying zone (feudal Europe) that this Italian expansion set fire to the grassland and accelerated the rate of evolution to the extent of creating in Europe a system that was qualitatively superior to that of the formerly more advanced societies. I have given (in *Class and Nation*) a detailed explanation of this conjuncture which establishes a link between the state's weakness and the establishment of an area of autonomy for a veritable new class – the middle class – to appear, then the state's alliance with the latter in order to go beyond the

Figure 3 The tributary systems (300 BC–1500 AD)

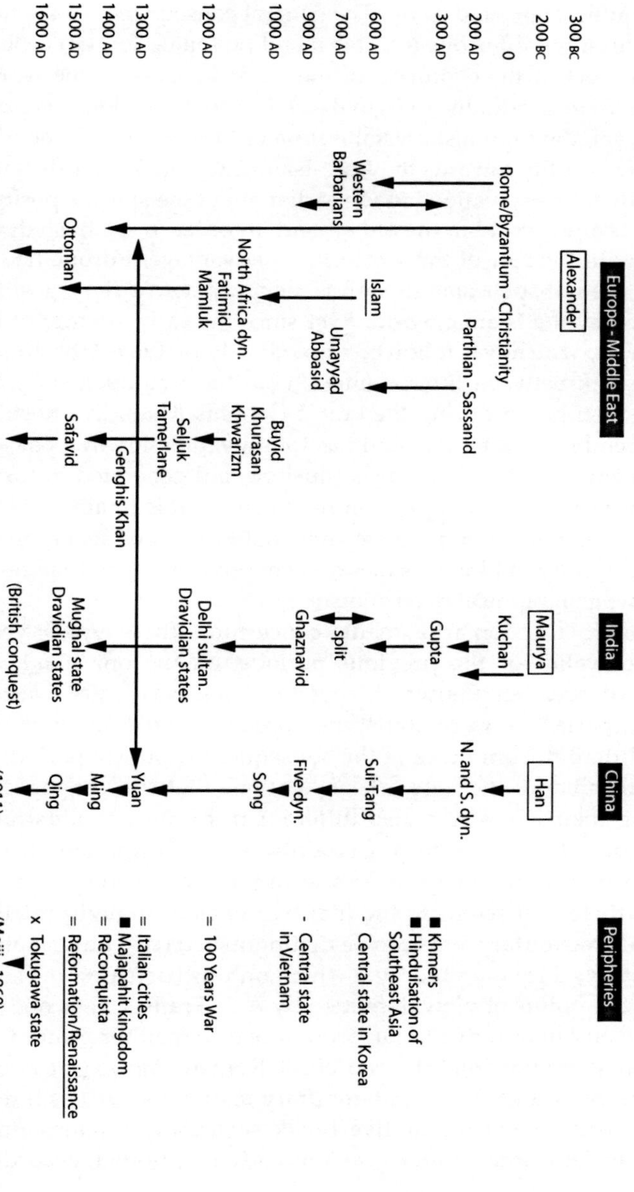

	Europe – Middle East	India	China	Peripheries
300 BC		Maurya	Han	■ Khmers
200 BC	Alexander			■ Hinduisation of Southeast Asia
0	Rome/Byzantium – Christianity			
200 AD		Kuchan	N. and S. dyn.	- Central state in Korea
300 AD	Parthian – Sassanid			
600 AD		Gupta	Sui–Tang	- Central state in Vietnam
700 AD	Islam			
	Umayyad Abbasid	split		
900 AD		Ghaznavid	Five dyn.	
1000 AD			Song	
1200 AD	North Africa dyn. Fatimid Mamluk	Delhi sultan. Dravidian states		= 100 Years War
	Buyid Khurasan Khwarizm		Yuan	
	Seljuk Tamerlane		Ming	= Italian cities
1300 AD	Genghis Khan			= Majapahit kingdom
	Safavid	Mughal state Dravidian states	Qing	= Reconquista
1400 AD				= Reformation/Renaissance
1500 AD	Ottoman			x Tokugawa state
1600 AD	Western Barbarians	(British conquest)	(1911)	(Meiji – 1860)

45

breaking up of the feudal system by creating a new absolutist and mercantilist state, and so on. The general consequence of the new crystallisation of Europe (capitalist and no longer feudal) is obvious: it blocked the evolution of the other societies of the world, which were gradually marginalised in the new global system. Moreover, the capitalist crystallisation of Europe brought about a specific hostility towards the Arab-Islamic region. We recall at this juncture the observation I made earlier about the specific position of the Islamic world in the old system. In order to establish direct links with the rest of the world to its advantage, Europe had to break the indispensable monopolistic and intermediary position enjoyed by the Islamic world. Ever since the early attempt of the Crusades, which was followed immediately by the establishment of the link between Europe and China that was opened by the Mongolian peace during the era of Genghis Khan, this hostility has been pursued to date and has found expression in a particularly neurotic attitude towards Muslims and generated in turn a similar response from the opposite direction. It is finally to break up this inevitable intermediate zone that Europeans set off on the seas. Contrary to Pirenne's thesis, such a choice was not the result of some geographical determinism.

Fourth, the remarks made concerning these 2,000 years are not valid for the previous periods: on the one hand, the civilised societies known during previous periods – a fortiori the barbarians – were sometimes organised in a manner that was different from those of the subsequent tributary period; on the other hand, the network of relations that they engaged in among themselves was also different from the one illustrated by Figure 1 and Figure 3. Certainly our scientific knowledge of the past becomes even less as we recede further in time. Nevertheless, it seems to me that two lines of thought relating to the 'pretributary' eras can be distinguished (two philosophies of history). Pirenne's theory – which on this basic point is similar to the points of view defended by A.G. Frank – does not recognise any qualitative break around 300 BC, neither around the Christian era nor from the end of the Roman empire (the end of Antiquity, according to contemporary textbooks), just as it does not recognise any qualitative break separating modern times from ancient times. Indeed, as I already mentioned, according to Pirenne, all periods of human history are marked by the same contrast between open, maritime and capitalistic societies and closed, landlocked and feudal societies. Moreover, like Frank, Pirenne emphasises the exchange relations that existed among the societies at all times, irrespective of the distance separating them (for example, on the exchanges between Sumer, the Indus civilisation, Egypt, Crete, Phoenicia and Greece). Like Frank, Pirennes theory is based on a philosophy of linear history: the progress is quantitative and continuous, without any qualitative change; in the words of Frank, it is the 'culmination of accumulation'. On the other hand, the commonly accepted theory of Marxism distinguishes three stages of civilisation that are different in terms of quality: slavery, feudalism and capitalism. I do not enter into this field of Marxology, to resolve the question of knowing whether this theory is really that of Marx (and of Engels) – and to what extent – or whether it is only that of the subsequent Marxian common understanding. In any case, this theory states that all the societies listed in Figure 3 are feudal societies: for Europe, from the end of the Roman empire; for the Byzantine and Islamic Middle East, right from their constitutions; for India, since the installation of the Maurya dynasty; and for China, since the Han era. Previously, on the other hand, according to this theory, they must have passed through a phase of slavery whose obvious and indisputable existence would be exemplified by Greece and Rome. In my opinion, people put forward by analogy a stage of slavery in China (from the Shang to the Han), in India (the Indus and Aryan civilisations), in the Middle East (in Mesopotamia). The existence of slavery located elsewhere and later on in certain regions of Africa, produced by the disintegration of earlier communal configurations, proves – according to this theory – that the passage through slavery constitutes a general requirement.

I do not share this point of view (see *Class and Nation*) and have offered instead a theory according to which: (1) the general form of class society that succeeded the previous communal formations is that of the tributary society; (2) the feudal form is not the general rule but only the peripheral form of the tributary type; (3) various conditions determine the specific form of each tributary society (castes, estates of the feudal era in the European sense – *Stände*; peasant communities subjected to a state bureaucracy, etc); (4) slavery is not a general requirement – it is absent from most of the landmarks of history (Egypt, India, China); it hardly undergoes any important development unless it is linked to a commercial economy and is therefore found within ages that are very different from the point of view of the development of productive forces (Graeco-Roman slavery and slavery in America up to the 19th century). Are the periods before the break of tributary societies which is marked in Figure 3 not then to be distinguished from the rest of the precapitalist history? For instance, Egypt in particular offers the example of a tributary society having practically nothing to do with slavery whose history begins 3,000 years before the crystallisation of the Hellenistic era. Assyria, Babylon, Iran of the Achemenids and probably pre-Mauryan India and pre-Han China sometimes practised slavery but this practice did not constitute the main form of exploitation of productive labour. Finally, according to my theory, a tributary society is not crystallised into its complete form until it produced a universal ideology – a religion based on universal values that go beyond the ideologies of kinship and country religions peculiar to the previous community stage. In this perspective, Zoroaster, Buddha and Confucius announce the crystallisation of the tributary society. Until then, I prefer to talk about 'incubation' or even the 'long transition from communal forms to the tributary form'. This transition, which is perhaps relatively simple and rapid in China, is made more complicated in India as a result of the Aryan invasion that destroyed the Indus civilisation. In the Middle East the diversity of the peoples and trajectories, as well as the mutual influence of one people by the other, compels us to consider the region as a system. I place within this context the early maturing of Egypt into a tributary society, the distinctive mercantile nature of slavery in Greece, and therefore I give particular importance to the Hellenistic synthesis, the prelude to the Christian and Islamic revolutions which were to take over the unification of the region.

Does the intensity of the exchange relations among the societies of these distant eras make it possible to talk about a 'system'? I doubt it, considering that the civilised societies, that is, those advanced in the transition to the tributary form, still remain islets in the ocean of worlds of communities. Even when they are parallel, the trajectories do not prove that the societies in question do constitute a system but establish only the validity of the general laws of evolution.

This chapter is an edited version of a paper that was first published in 1991 as 'The ancient world systems versus the modern capitalist world system', Review, vol. XIV, no. 3, pp. 349–85.

References

Amin, Samir (1978) *The Arab Nation*, London, Zed Books
——(1980) *Class and Nation, Historically and in the Current Crisis*, New York, Monthly Review Press
——(2010) *Eurocentrism* (2nd edition), Oxford, Pambazuka Press
Fawzy, Mansour (1990) L'impasse du monde arabe, les racines historique, Paris, L'Harmattan
Frank, André Gunder (1990) 'A theoretical introduction to 5,000 years of world system history', *Review*, vol. XIII, no. 2 (Spring), pp. 155–48
Pirenne, Jacques (1948) *Les grands courants de l'histoire universelle*, 4 vols, Neuchatel, Editions de la Baconnière
Polanyi, Karl (1987) *La Liberta in una societa complesse*, Milan, Boringheri
Sadek Saad, Ahmad *Rarikh Misr al Ijtimai*
Toynbee, Arnold (1962) *A Study of History*, 12 vols, Oxford, Oxford University Press

2

Central Asia and the Middle East in the tributary system of the ancient world

In the first chapter, I proposed considering the societies of the ancient world for the whole period of 2,000 years as an ensemble of societies that had common characteristics, which I called the central and peripheral forms of the tributary mode of production, articulated between themselves in a system of flourishing exchanges of all kinds. I refer the reader to that chapter for the conceptual systems proposed for analysing the specificity of this tributary mode, in contrast with that of modern capitalism, as well as for the analysis of the function of inter-regional trade. I summed up my conclusion in Figure 1 and Figures 2 and 3. The volumes of trade between the centres and peripheries, as designated in Table 1, and that of the transit through Central Asia (the Silk Routes) were estimated for each of the great routes, indicated by the 11 arrows in Figure 1.

This period stretches over almost 20 centuries, during the course of which it is clear that there was an evolution in the relative importance of each of the defined regions (centres A, B and C and the peripheries), as also, therefore, in their foreign trade. The indices both for the volume of the surplus generated in the region and for trade as well as the distribution of these according to the arrows in Figure 1 varied over the course of time. I will therefore now present the justification of the averages retained to describe this long historical period.

China was not only the most important centre over the whole period, but the one whose development was the most continuous, in spite of the disorders that occurred in the inter-dynastic periods.

The population of China was 70 million inhabitants at the

beginning of the Christian era (28 per cent of the world population at the time, which was 250 million). It grew regularly to reach 200 million in 1700 (which was still 28 per cent of the world population, estimated at 680 million). Between 1700 and 1800 the demographic trend accelerated and the Chinese population reached 330 million, representing 35 per cent of the world population, estimated at 950 million.

Over the course of this long period, China was the most advanced in all fields. It had the greatest agricultural productivity per capita, the largest number of towns that provided a base for an educated administrative population, with skilled artisans. It was considered by everyone as something of a model: when the Europeans discovered it in the 18th century, which was the century of its greatest splendour, they were greatly inspired by it (see Étiemble, *L'Europe chinoise*). Much earlier, the peoples of the Middle East were aware of its wealth and power (see the *hadith* of the Prophet Mohamed: 'go and seek science in China').

For this reason I chose 100 as the index to indicate the volume of foreign trade of China throughout the period. On the hypothesis that this trade would have taken up 10 per cent of the surplus generated in China, the latter could be given an index of 1,000 (for a population that regularly grew from 50 to 330 million).

Over the whole of this period China maintained close, continual and substantial relationships with the Middle Eastern centre (Hellenistic, then Byzantine and Islamic – Arab, Persian and Turkish). I suggest estimating this volume of trade at two-thirds (65 per cent) of all Chinese trade for the whole period, as against 20 per cent with Japan, 5 per cent with Southeast Asia and 10 per cent with Europe. What are the indices on which I have based these estimates?

The Middle East centre had a very different history. In 200 BC it had a population about the same as that of China (50 million) and probably its general level of development was at least equal. But at the beginning of the Christian era its population was only 35 million (as against 70 million for China), using a limited definition of the region (Greece–Anatolia, Egypt, Syria–Iraq–Iran). If one adds Italy and the Maghreb, which constitute its prolongation towards the west, associated with the construction of the Roman empire, the population would come to 50 million. For the following centuries the population of the Middle East centre (Byzantium plus the Caliphate) remained relatively stagnant. The population of the heirs of the Ottoman empire as from 1500, the Persian empire and the Emirates and Khanates of Turkish Central Asia barely exceeded 50 million compared to more than 200 million in China and as many in India in 1700. The relative decline of the Middle East has been virtually continuous since the Christian era, in spite of brilliant, but short, moments when efforts were made to renew it (in the Justinian era, the first two Abbasid centuries).

In contrast, the relative position of the Middle East in still older times had been dominant at the world level. During the 2,000 years preceding the Christian era its population represented perhaps 30 per cent of the world's total inhabitants (which grew very slowly from 100 to 250 million during this period) compared with only 18 per cent at the time of the Christian era and 7 per cent in 1700. Ancient Egypt had a population that exceeded 10 million, but this figure fell to 2 million in 1800, only recovering its level of pharaonic times in the 20th century. This is not the place to discuss the reasons for this relatively early and inexorable decline, but it should be mentioned that it was accentuated by the enormous devastation in Central Asia, Iran and Iraq caused by the Turko-Mongolian invasions that reduced Iran and Mesopotamia, one of the cradles of universal civilisation, to desolate steppes. Russia and the Islamic Orient were the main victims of these invasions, China having been far more capable of resisting them. Nevertheless it is a fact that, as from the Christian era, the Middle East centre never experienced a dynamism comparable to that of China.

Trade between China and the Middle East was relatively greater in ancient times, then subsequently declining, with the difference being made up – for China – by increased trade with Korea and Japan, Vietnam and Southeast Asia and, finally, Europe, at first along the Mongolian route (13th century), then by sea (in modern times).

The relative stagnation of the Middle East indicated that the surplus generated in this region was comparable to that of China at the beginning of the period under consideration (as from 50 BC), but it was barely one-third of China's surplus towards 1300–1500, taking into account the demographic evolutions of both populations. The median between these two extreme indices – 1,000 and

350 – at around 700, is slightly less than the 800 figure indicated in our diagram for the whole period.

The declining position of the Middle East has nevertheless been partially offset by its geographical location, which is that of a crossroads, an obligatory intermediary for almost all transcontinental trade in the pre-modern epochs. This is the reason for the degree of commercialisation of the economy and a volume of external trade that is relatively impressive: about 20 per cent, perhaps, as opposed to 10 per cent for China. This proportion – of 2:1 – is consistent with the comparative estimates of trade between the Middle East region and the other regions of the pre-modern world (see below).

The extent of trade between China and the Middle East, although in decline in relative terms, remained the outstanding characteristic of the system of relations between the regions of the pre-modern world. This transfer of goods, technologies, ideologies and religions facilitated, with the Middle East as intermediary, the dissemination of the most advanced Chinese science and technology, particularly towards Europe.

The route that was followed from time immemorial was known as the Silk Route, which left China through the Gansu corridor, passing south of the Tian Shan mountain range, running alongside the desert of Taklamatan, either to the north of it (Hami-Aksu-Kashgar), or to the south of it (Kokand-Kashgar) and then going towards Persia through the south of former Soviet central Asia (Samarkand-Bokhara-Khiva).

The enduring nature of this vital route explains many phenomena that would otherwise be difficult to understand, like the early and deep penetration of religions coming from the Middle East: Christian Nestorianism, Zarathustrian Manicheism (people forget that central Asia was Christianised before the German tribes), then Islam (which immediately put down solid roots in this region, in the Khorezm) and from India (Buddhism). This penetration accompanied the early settlement of the local populations: from the 9th century eastern Turkestan (now the Uighur Autonomous Region) was completely settled. From the frontiers of China itself to those of Persia, the route was studded with large commercial towns, centres of intellectual activity, surrounded by zones of intensive, irrigated agriculture.

It is thus easy to comprehend that the main geostrategic conflict of pre-modern times is aimed at the control of this route. It is in fact striking that the military frontier between the region under Chinese control and that under the control of the Middle East (the Caliphate and Persia) remained remarkably stable, close to what are now the Chinese frontiers. It is also remarkable that, in spite of its Islamisation, eastern Turkestan has always been under Chinese political and military control, while western Turkestan was under the control of the Middle East (when it had not actually taken over power in that region) before being conquered by the Russians.

The relative decline in trade between China and the Middle East was, as we have said, offset by the increase, late but considerable, in trade with Korea, Japan, Vietnam and Southeast Asia. At the beginning of the Christian era, these regions were only thinly populated (1 million for Korea and Japan, 6 for Southeast Asia – altogether less than one-tenth of the Chinese population at the time). It was not before the second half of the first millennium that centralised states were established in this region, inspired, in fact, by the Chinese model. But progress was rapid, even though the demographic increase remained inferior to that of China. Working on the hypothesis of a growing volume of trade that paralleled the statistics of the populations concerned, at the end of the period (which extended beyond 1500 up to almost 1800) one gets an index that is equal to that of the trade between China and the Middle East. On the other hand these relationships between China and the Middle East stretched over the 20 centuries under consideration (gradually declining in relative terms), whereas the relationships between China and Europe developed in the six last centuries of the tributary period. The average index is therefore about a third of that affecting the first ones, some 25 (against 65), distributed mainly to the benefit of Japan (20), then to Southeast Asia (5). The index for China/Europe trade (without passing through the Middle East) was 10 and will be justified later on.

India constituted the second centre of human concentration and civilisation, after China. Its civilisation took off very early, during the third millennium BC; in other words, in the same period as Egypt and Mesopotamia with which, in fact, the civilisations of the Indus Valley were perhaps in contact.

Like China and unlike the Middle East, India experienced a

2 CENTRAL ASIA AND THE MIDDLE EAST

continuous dynamism from its origins up to 1700. It had a population of 45 million at the dawn of the Christian era and 200 million in 1700 (the same as China at that time). But then it entered into crisis. By 1800 it had made no headway, remaining at about 200 million and it did not pick up again until later, in the 19th century. The Indian (sub)continent still today constitutes the largest concentration of humanity after China.

For the period we are considering (from 500 BC, with the appearance of Buddha, up until the 16th century, which saw the beginning of European maritime control over the Indian Ocean), we can therefore accept the hypothesis of the surplus generated in the region as equivalent to that produced in China (the same index of 1,000), because of the high productivity of its agriculture and its flourishing towns.

Nevertheless, the history of India is more chaotic than that of China. It was frequently invaded (always from the west) and it was difficult to unify (this only happened in the ancient period of the Mauryan empire, in the early part of our period). According to all the historians it was less open to foreign trade than China. Its trade was in fact above all with the Middle East, partly by land through Iran and Afghanistan and partly by sea. As for its trade with Southeast Asia, this did not become important until the Hinduisation epoch of the latter, between the years 600 and 1000, which was then followed by the Islamisation of Indonesia and Malaysia and intensifying penetration by the Chinese.

If, as we justify later on, the index of India/Middle East trade can be estimated at 50 for the whole period under consideration (half of the trade carried out on land and half by sea), and that of India/Southeast Asia estimated at 10, the foreign trade percentage of the surplus would come to 6 per cent, less than that of China which, as we saw, was 10 per cent. This result is consistent with the views of the historians referred to earlier.

Europe did not participate in the general development of the pre-modern system until very late, after the year 1000. Up until then it had remained a backward and barbarous periphery.

At the dawn of the Christian era the population of Europe, including Italy, was about 20 million (8 per cent of the world population, less than 30 per cent of that of China, 50 per cent of that of the Middle East). Half of the Europeans lived in Italy and in Gaul. At first, the take-off of Europe was very slow because in the year 1000 there were hardly more than 30 million inhabitants, including Italy. After that, however, the increase was rapid: between the years 1000 and 1350 the population reached 80 million (18 per cent of the world population, estimated at 440 million). It then diminished to 60 million in 1400 (because of the Black Death), but increased again to reach 120 million in 1700 (18 per cent of the world population, calculated at 950 million). The European population then began to rise rapidly, exploding in the 19th century.

Until the year 1000 the productivity of European agriculture was greatly inferior to that of the civilised regions of China, India and the Middle East, and the continent still had no towns. The take-off was rapid from then on, however, and two centuries later Europe was covered with lively towns and monuments that showed the growth of the surplus that its agriculture had generated. For the two or three last centuries of the period we are considering, which closed in 1492 with the start of the world hegemony of modern and capitalist Europe, the continent represented a new centre, with a relative weight equal to half of that of China and it was already double or triple that of the Middle East. This is if one accepts the hypothesis, which is probable, that agricultural productivity is equivalent to the degree of urbanisation.

In contrast, for some 15 centuries preceding this time, Europe was hardly present in the world system of the period because the low productivity of labour made it impossible to extract much surplus: the index of this surplus could have been close to zero, but it rose quickly to an index of 350 (a third of that of China) for the centuries 1200–1500. The median (or weighted average) of 100 (see Figure 1) for the whole of this long period could be misleading here, as for Japan and Southeast Asia, and even more so than for the latter because it claims to illustrate rapid, though tardy growth.

The volume of Europe's foreign trade, estimated at an index of 20, does in fact apply only to the period of four centuries, 1100–1500, as trade before then was negligible. In this period the population of Europe was between a third and a half of that of China. It is therefore possible that this index is somewhat underestimated if one takes only that period of four centuries into consideration. However, it is certainly greatly overestimated if it is applied to the long period of 300 BC to 1500 AD.

Most of the commerce passed through the Middle East, even if many of the products imported by Europe came from further afield, from China or India, and only transited the Middle East. In the 13th century, however, for the first time, direct contact was established between Europe and China by the Mongolian land route, avoiding the Middle East. The after effects of Genghis Khan's conquests occurred at precisely the time when Europe was taking off and rapidly catching up the three more advanced regions constituted by the three oriental centres. Trade between Europe and China was therefore intensive, although the period when the Mongolian route was used was very brief – less than a century. In fact, as from 1500 the sea route supplanted the old land routes. The index for this trade (10) would certainly be overestimated if one had to establish the volume over the whole of the long period being considered. Hence the misplaced appreciation of the conquests of Genghis Khan by the Europeans when they discovered the existence of China. For the dominant discourse, Eurocentric as always, attributed the positive role of the Mongol empire in establishing the East–West contact which had already been in existence for a long time, even if the Europeans were unaware of the fact. On the contrary, the negative effect of the Turko-Mongolian conquests, which impoverished the most important trade partners of the past, through the massive devastations in northern China, south-west Central Asia, Iran and Iraq, as well as Russia, has always been underestimated in this Eurocentric viewpoint. On the whole the Mongolian conquests were more negative than positive as far as East–West trade was concerned.

Even during the last centuries of the long period we are considering, Europe, which was on the periphery of the old system, lagged behind. This is evident from the European balance of trade, which was also greatly in deficit, as the continent did not have much to offer: for its imports of luxury goods and technology from the East it could only make up their deficit by exporting metal.

The estimate proposed for the indices of the volume of surplus generated in the peripheries of sub-Saharan Africa and South Asia is based on the estimates of the population statistics for these regions: they had about half the European population at the dawn of the Christian era, not a very dynamic demographic growth, low agricultural productivity and no urbanisation worthy of the name, as in Europe up until the year 1000.

As we did for Europe, we consider that the low productivity rate meant that the surplus generated was, compared with the more advanced regions, less than proportional to the population statistics. On the other hand, it is precisely because the modest surplus is traded for luxury goods that are foreign to local production, that the degree of extreme commercialisation of this surplus is higher, for distant trade is relatively more important than that closer to home. This is why the figure is around 20 per cent (as against 10 per cent in China and 6 per cent in India) for Europe (surplus: 100, foreign trade: 20), 20 per cent also for Africa (surplus: 50, foreign trade: 10) and even 30 per cent for Southeast Asia (surplus: 60, foreign trade: 20).

Sub-Saharan Africa was not, as Arabic writings show, a periphery that was more miserable than Europe before the 11th century. Africa began to fall behind later, in comparison with Europe when the latter took off and the lateness of the former was exacerbated by the massive destruction wreaked by the Atlantic slave trade – not only the devastating effects on the demography of the continent, but also the political degeneration that accompanied it (destruction of the large states that were being formed, which were substituted by military predator states).

Southeast Asia started, at the beginning of our long period, from a peripheral position comparable to that of Europe and sub-Saharan Africa. It initiated a certain progress before Europe, with its Hinduisation (succeeded by Islamisation), as from the 7th century, which brought about intensive trade with India and more modest trade with China and the Middle East. This growth was not brutally interrupted until the 16th century when the European maritime hegemony began to break up the old commercial ties. However, perhaps because it did not undergo the ravages of slavery like Africa, its position did not deteriorate in the same way.

We can now return to the Middle East, the crossroads of premodern trade, to recapitulate its flows, the indices of which were then the following: trade with China (65), India (50), Africa (10), Europe (10) and Southeast Asia (5). The total amount of these flows – 140 – represented 20 per cent of the surplus generated locally, if the index 800 is accepted. If this index is too high, taking into account the relative stagnation of the region in comparison with the permanent dynamism of China and India, as well as the late but vigorous growth of Europe, the percentage of the surplus commercialised in foreign trade would be still higher. In fact this relationship is stretching it somewhat because part of the merchandise was only in transit. In ancient times, when the Middle East was a centre comparable in weight to China and India, most of the trade (and it was at that time most of the trade at the world level) was not transit commerce. On the other hand, when Europe began its take-off after the year 1000 certainly a good part of the trade coming from China and India only transited through the Middle East.

What we have just said about the Middle East is even truer, if we consider the Central Asia region, whose position was neither that of a centre or of a periphery.

Central Asia was an obligatory passage between the main pre-modern centres, particularly between China and the Middle East. It had always been sparsely populated, thus itself producing only a negligible surplus. Our index of 60, purely indicative here, is probably overestimated even if, at certain periods the region of south-west Turkestan, around the waterways of the Syr and Amu Darya, experienced brilliant development. Nevertheless the trade flows passing through the region were considerable, as indicated by their total indices (100). More than any other region in the world, Central Asia benefited from this transit, as a proportion of its value, doubtless impossible to estimate but it must have been considerable, remained in the region.

Nevertheless it is important not to make too many generalisations about this region, which has never been either homogenous or limited to nomadism. In fact, Central Asia is roughly divided by the Tian Shan range into a southern region – the real Silk Route – and a northern region which has only ever been marginal in East–West exchanges, which have been intensive since at least the 6th century BC.

The southern part of the region is itself clearly divisible into three distinct sub-regions: eastern Turkestan (the Chinese autonomous region of Sinkiang), western Turkestan, south of the present Kazakhstan, and Afghanistan.

Two-thirds of the trade flows crossing central Asia, corresponding to China–Middle East trade, always took the same route, passing through Sinkiang and the Syr and Amu Darya valleys. Any variations of this route, to avoid the desert of Taklamatan to the north or the south, used the Dzungaria route or the mountain passes leading to the Fergana Valley, which are all situated in this region.

The eastern part of southern Central Asia (Sinkiang) is particularly dry, with only a scattering of oases, which hinders any density of population, except in urban areas. For these oasis towns were able to get their food supplies both from small areas of irrigated land in their immediate proximity and from transiting long-distance commerce. It has therefore never been a question in this region of a social formation that was predominantly nomadic, but rather of urban/traders. But this would not exist were it not for the East–West relationships, onto which it had been grafted. Sometimes the local powers benefit from an autonomy that was close to independence; at others they were strictly subordinated to Chinese rule. In both cases the social formation was only a sub-system of articulation between the tributary formations of China and the Middle East. This objective dependency did not impair the importance of the region and the brilliance of its civilisation, marked by an early and total sedentarisation (going back at least to the 9th century) and by the intellectual life of its open urban centres (which, for this reason easily adopted the advanced forms of religion with a universalistic outlook, like Nestorianism, Manicheism, Buddhism and Islam).

To the west of the mountain barrier separating Sinkiang from western Turkestan, the geographical conditions permitted both a more numerous nomad population of the steppes and irrigated agriculture around the Syr and Amu Darya rivers. The region was a kind of prolongation of the Iranian plateau and the Afghan massif and an excellent example of contacts between the sedentary (cultivators and urbanites) and the nomads. According to the vagaries of history, the social formations of the region were therefore either urban-trading (supported by irrigated agriculture) or nomadic. Obviously East–West trade was more stimulated in the former case, hindered in the latter. The Turko-Mongolian invasions were never – contrary to a widespread belief – conducive to this commerce.

Afghanistan has a special place in this regional system. India always maintained close relations with the Middle East which, as well as the sea route, took a route passing through the north of the Afghan massif, thus joining, on the Amu Daria, the Chinese–Middle East highway. In this triple contact (Middle East–India–China), civilisations that were a particularly interesting synthesis (like the Quchan state) were able to flourish. Trade between India and China also passed through here to avoid the uncrossable barrier of the Himalayas and Tibet, skirting around them to the west. This was the route taken by Buddhism.

The northern half of the Asian interior roughly corresponds to present Mongolia (to the north of Tian Shan) and the steppes of Kazakhstan (to the north of the Aral Sea and the Syr Darya), which stretch without hindrance to the centre of Europe, passing north of the Caspian and Black seas. This region has only played a minor role in East–West relations for at least two reasons: the backwardness of Europe up until the year 1000 and the dominance of the turbulent nomadic population of the steppes. As we saw, this northern route was only taken during the short period between the European take-off, starting in the 12th century, and the conquest of the seas, starting in the 16th century, which corresponds to the conquest of the whole region by Genghis Khan.

The dominant social formation here was different from those prevailing in the southern half of the region. Nomadism, which was predominant, was linked with impoverished trading – although it in no way compared with the intensity of such relationships along the real Silk Route. Mongolia has no traces of important towns and even at the time of Genghis Khan the capital Karakorum was a market town of possibly 5,000 inhabitants. There was also no comparison with the towns of southern Central Asia, because the main East–West trade did not pass through Mongolia. Also, the trade between China and the regions situated to the north of Tian Shan – Mongolia and Siberia – continued to be extremely restricted, virtually limited to the importation by China of horses and furs. Control of the trade by China of the Qing, after the collapse of the Genghis Khanate of Mongolia, built a new nomadic articulation, Buddhist feudalism–Chinese mercantilism, which was dominant from the 16th to the 20th century. At the same time the Russian expansion in Siberia brought a new conflict of geopolitical control between the Russians and the Chinese. Russia, however, did not then – it was already the modern epoch – represent the heart of European capitalism, but rather a poor semi-periphery. Its foreign trade was therefore of little importance.

The reference here to the role of Buddhism in Mongolian social formation raises an issue that deserves to be studied more in depth. It is striking to see the failure of Buddhism in the centres of Asian civilisations: in India, its country of origin, in China where Hinduism and Confucianism rapidly overwhelmed it, and along the Silk Routes where Islam had established itself. However, Buddhism took definite root in the two marginal regions of Central Asia, in Tibet and Mongolia.

To the west of Mongolia, the northern region of the Asian interior remained, as we have said, without precise limits, including Kazakhstan and southern Russia. It is in this region that the invading nomads, who had all, or almost all, been gradually Islamised (but without this conversion, late as it was, having any deep cultural effects), came up against the no less invasive Russians.

The global structure of the tributary system over the 20 centuries under consideration was characterised by a remarkable stability, which legitimises Figure 1 as an illustration of this stability. This was of relative importance in each of the regional blocs, for in population and in wealth there were evolutions that gradually upset the relations between these blocs and created the new structure that was characteristic of modern capitalism. At risk of repeating myself, I stress that the index figures that I have used to quantify the listed trade flows represent the averages over the long period under consideration, which do not therefore correspond exactly to any of the sub-periods. For each of these we would therefore have to have a system of specific index figures, showing the relative importance of the regions at that epoch.

I recapitulate the most significant characteristics of this evolution, as follows:

1. For this whole period of 20 centuries, China's progress was continuous and sustained. The position of this country-continent therefore remained remarkably stable (although not dominant, see above) in the system of the tributary ancient

world. The same could be said, to a lesser degree, of India, the second country-continent of the system.

2. In contrast, the stagnation of the Middle East for the whole of the period fatally reflected the clear regression of its position in the system.

3. The most striking evolution was in Europe. A marginal periphery for 15 centuries, Europe made tremendous progress, in terms of its pace, during the five centuries preceding the capitalist revolution. This upheaval became even more marked in the two centuries following the period under study, through the conquest and shaping of America by Europe and the inauguration of the transforming of a system that had previously only concerned the ancient world into a total global system.

4. The evolutions in other regions (Japan, Southeast Asia, Africa) also prepared, in their own way, for the setting up of a new, global capitalist system.

5. The capitalist system which was established as from 1500 AD. is qualitatively different from the preceding system. It was not only a question of the disruption in the relative positions of the regions concerned, to the profit of Europe. The latter constituted itself as the dominant centre at the global level, a centre that would be augmented by the European expansion in North America and by the emergence of Japan. The concept of domination that now characterises the new world system did not exist in the previous tributary system. I have stressed, in association with this transformation, the importance of another transformation, no less qualitative: the transfer of dominance in the social system of the politico-ideological instance to the economy.

6. Central Asia had been a key region in the ancient system, the obligatory passage linking the more advanced regions of the old epochs (China, India, the Middle East – to which Europe was added later). The studies of the region have emphasised the decisive importance of the interactions and commercial, scientific, technological exchanges which have passed through this key region. Central Asia lost these functions in the world capitalist system and, for this reason, was to be definitively marginalised.

This chapter is an edited version of a chapter that was first published in 1996 as 'Le role de l'Asie centrale dans le système tributaire de l'ancien monde') in Les défis de la mondialisation, *Paris, L'Harmattan.*

Bibliography

Abu-Lughod, Janet (1989) *Before European Hegemony: The World System* AD *1250–1350*, New York, Oxford University Press

Amin, Samir (1989) *Eurocentrism: Modernity, Religion and Democracy – A Critique of Eurocentrism and Culturlaism* (2nd edn), Oxford, Pambazuka Press

Arrighi, Giovanni (1994) *The Long Twentieth Century*, London and New York, Verso

Ashtor, E.A. (1976) *Social and Economic History of the Near East in the Middle Ages*, London, Collins

Bartjold, W. (1947) *Histoire des Turcs d'Asie central*, Paris, Maisonneuve

Beckwith, Christopher (1989) *The Tibetan Empire in Central Asia*, Princeton, NJ, Princeton University Press

Bernal, Martin (1987) *Black Athena: The Afro-Asiatic Roots of Classical Civilization*, New Brunswick, Rutgers University Press

Blaut, J.M. (1989) 'Colonialism and the rise of capitalism', *Science and Society*, vol 53, no. 3

——(1991) *Fourteen Ninety-Two: The Debate on Colonialism, Eurocentrism and History*, Trenton, NJ, Africa World Press

Braudel, Fernand (1967–79) *Civilisation matérielle, économie et capitalisme XV-XVIIe siècle*, 3 vols, Paris, Armand Colin

Ceodes, G. (1948) *Les Etats hindouisés d'Indochine et d'Indonésie*, Paris, Ed. de Brocard

Chase Dunn, Christopher and Hall, Thomas D. (eds) (1991) *Core/Periphery Relations in Precapitalist Worlds*, Boulder, CO, Westview Press

——(1991) *World-Systems and Modes of Production*, Vancouver, ISA

Chaudhuri, K.N. (1985) *Trade and Civilization in the Indian Ocean: An Economic History from the Rise of Islam to 1750*, Cambridge, Cambridge University Press

de St Croix, G.E.M. (1981) *The Class Struggle in the Ancient Greek World*, London, Duckworth

Ekholm, Kajsa (1982) 'Capitalism, imperialism and exploitation in ancient world systems', *Review*, vol. 4, no.1

Etiemble, R. (1988) *L'Europe chinoise*, Paris, Gallimard

Fitzpatrick, John (1991) Wars, States and Markets in North East Asia 800–1400 AD, Vancouver, ISA

Frank, André Gunder (1978) *World Accumulation 1492–1789*, Monthly Review Press

——(1990) 'A theoretical introduction to 5,000 years of world systems history', *Review*, vol. 8, no. 2

——(1991) 'Transitional ideological modes: feudalism, capitalism, socialism', *Critique of Anthropology*, vol II, no. 2

Friedman, Edward (ed) (1982) *Ascent and Decline in the World System*, Beverly Hills, Sage

Gernet, Jacques (1985) *A History of China*, Cambridge, Cambridge University Press

Ghirshman, R. (1954) *Iran*, London, Pelican, Penguin Books

Gills, B.K. and Frank, A.G. (1990) 'The cumulation of accumulation: theses and research agenda for 5,000 years of world system history', *Dialectical Anthropology*, vol. 15, no. 1, pp. 19–42. Also in Chase-Dunn, C. and Hall, T. (eds) (1991) *Core/Periphery Relations in Precapitalist Worlds*, Boulder, CO, Westview Press

Goldstein, Joshua S. (1988) *Long Cycles. Prosperity and War in the Modern Age*, New Haven, CT, Yale University Press,

Grousset, René (1947) *L'Empire des steppes*, Paris, Payot

Hodgson, Marshall G.S. (1974) *The Venture of Islam*, 3 vols, Chicago, IL, University of Chicago Press

Humphreys, S.C. (1978) *History, Economics and Anthropology: the World of Karl Polanyi*, London, Routledge and Kegan Paul

Kohl, Philip L. (1978) 'The balance of trade in Southwestern Asia in the mid-third millennium', *Current Anthropology*, vol. 19, no. 3.

——(1987) 'The ancient economy, transferable technologies and the Bronze Age world system: a view from the northeastern frontier of the Ancient Near East', in Rowlands, M., Larsen, M. and Kristansen, K. (eds) *Centre and Periphery in the Ancient World*, Cambridge, Cambridge University Press

——(1990) 'The use and abuse of world systems theory: the case of the pristine West Asian state', in Lamberg-Karlovsky, C.C. (ed) *Archeological Thought in America*, Cambridge, Cambridge University Press

Kwanten, Luc (1970) *Imperial Nomad*, Leicester, Leicester University Press

Liu, Xinru (1988) *Ancient India and Ancient China: Trade and Religious Exchanges AD 1600*, Delhi, Oxford University Press

Liverani, Mario (1987) 'The collapse of the near eastern regional system at the end of the Bronze Age: the case of Syria', in Rowlands, M., Larsen, M. and Kristansen, K. (eds) *Centre and Periphery in the Ancient World*, Cambridge, Cambridge University Press

Lombard, Maurice (1971) *L'Islam dans sa première grandeur*, Paris, Flammarion

Marfoe, Léon (1998) 'Cedar Forest to Silver Mountain: social change and the development of long distance trade in early Near Eastern societies', in Rowlands, M., Larsen, M. and Kristansen, K. (eds), *Centre and Periphery in the Ancient World*, Cambridge, Cambridge University Press

McNeill, William (1963) *The Rise of the West. A History of the Human Community*, Chicago, University of Chicago Press

——(1982) *The Pursuit of Power: Technology, Armed Force and Society Since AD 1000*, Chicago, University of Chicago Press

Melko, Matthew (1990) 'State systems in harmonious conflicts', paper presented at the annual meeting of the Japan Society for the Comparative Study of Civilisations, Kokugaluin University, Tokyo, December

Modelski, George (1987) *Long Cycles in World Politics*, London, Macmillan Press

Oates, Joan (1978), 'The balance of trade in southwestern Asia in the mid-third millennium' (comment on Philip Kohl), *Current Anthropology*, vol. 19, no. 3

Oppenheim, A. Leo and Reiner, Erica (1977), *Ancient Mesopotamia*, Chicago IL, University of Chicago Press

Palat, Ravi Arvind and Wallerstein, Immanuel (1990) 'Of what world system was pre-1500 "India" a part?', paper presented at the International Colloquium on 'Merchants, Companies and Trade', Maison des Sciences de l'Homme, Paris, 30 May–2 June 1990

Pirenne, Jacques (1947) *Les grands courants de l'histoire universelle*, Paris, Albin Michel

Polanyi, Karl (1957) *Trade and Markets in Early Empires*, Glencoe, The Free Press

Rossabi, Morris (1982) *China Among Equals: the Middle Kingdom and its Neighbors 10–14 Centuries*, Berkeley, University of California Press

Rostovtzeff, M. (1941) *The Economic and Social History of the Hellenistic World*, Oxford, Oxford University Press

Roux, George A. (1992) *Ancient Iraq*, Harmondsworth, Penguin Books

Rowlands, Michael, Larsen, Mogens and Kristansen, Kristian (eds) (1987) *Centre and Periphery in the Ancient World*. Cambridge University Press

Siver, Morris (1985) *Economic Structures of the Ancient Near East*, London, Croom Helm

Suziki, Chusei (1968) 'China's relations with inner Asia: the Hsiung-nu, Tibet', in Fairbank, John King (ed) *The Chinese World Order: Traditional China's Foreign Relations*, Cambridge, MA, Harvard University Press

Teggart, Frederick (1939) *Rome and China. A Study of Correlations in Historical Events*, Berkeley, CA, University of California Press

Thapar, Romila A. (1966) *A History of India*, Harmondsworth, Penguin Books

Toynbee, Arnold (1947) *A Study of History*, 6 vols, Oxford, Oxford University Press

Vladimirostov, B. (1948) *Le régime social des Mongols. Le féodalisme nomade*, Paris, Maisonneuve

Vernadsky, George (1969) *A History of Russia, 1943–1969*, 6 vols, New Haven, CT, Yale University Press

I would also like to draw attention to the three main sources from which I have drawn the population figures in this study:

Jean Claude Chesnais (1991) *La population du monde, de l'Antiquité à 2050*, Paris, Bordas

Jacques Vallin (1989) *La population mondiale*, Paris, Collection Repères, La Découverte

Tertius Chandler and Gérald Fox (1974) *3000 Years of Urban Growth*, New York, Academic Press

3

The challenge of globalisation

There is undoubtedly a fairly broad consensus regarding the principal characteristics of the challenge facing contemporary societies, at least regarding the following four points:

1. Since the beginning of the 1970s the economic system has been in a long period of relative stagnation (in comparison with the post-war phase of exceptional growth). Whether or not one terms our age as the downward swing of a Kondratieff cycle, the fact remains that rates of growth and investment in the expansion of systems of production have been lower for the last 20 years than they were during the two preceding decades. The entry of the system into this long-term stagnation has put an end to the illusions that were created by the previous period: that of full employment and indefinite growth in the West, that of development in the South, and that of 'catching up' through socialism in the East.

2. The dominant economic actors of the current day – large multinational firms – are capable of developing global strategies of their own, which to a great extent free them from the tutelage of states' national policies (whose impotence is recognised by both those who deplore it and those who rejoice in it). The economic system has become much more globalised than it was 30 years ago.

3. Financial preoccupations have gradually assumed more importance than those concerning economic growth or the expansion of systems of production. For some, this 'financialisation' of capital encourages usurious behaviour with negative consequences for economic and social development. It is therefore largely responsible for the longevity of stagnation and the severity of unemployment, as it locks

67

economic policies into a deflationary spiral. For others, it is both necessary and desirable as it conditions the restructuring of systems of production and thus paves the way for a new period of growth.

4. Finally, on the ideological and political levels the fundamental concepts of a socialist alternative – better socially and at least as effective economically as capitalism – based on a delinking from the global system, are once again being questioned: some deplore this fact and simply attribute the failures of experience to errors in putting the theory into practice (while the theoretical principles remain sound); others make a much more radical criticism of such attempts and consider that the strategy which defined them no longer corresponds to contemporary challenges; some, finally, welcome the failure as it comfortingly confirms that any attempt to reject capitalism is utopian.

The first three characteristics of the current crisis are not altogether new developments. The history of capitalism has already seen long periods of stagnation, phases of intensified financialisation and even globalisation; this is attributed to the fact that economic agents active outside the frontiers of their country escape its laws. None of this is without precedent. I show below, however, that some of these characteristics are presenting new aspects. The fourth of the above characteristics is, of course, clearly more recent.

However, if agreement exists around what we could call the broad realities of our age as outlined here, there are certainly fundamental divergences as soon as we study the analyses of these phenomena and the perspectives that they open (or close). These divergences not only divide the left (which includes social reformists, Keynesians and all those who declare themselves the inheritors of Marxism) and the right (defined by its adherence to the fundamental theses of neoclassical economics) but also cut across the two wings. As ever, when put to the test by developments which qualitatively change structures and thus fundamental behaviours, social thought is forced to redefine itself and to rethink the paradigmatic framework in which it situates the relationships between economic laws (and the constraining objectivity of their nature) and societal changes.

The dominant social thought is economistic in the sense which sets off from the idea that there are economic laws which are 'incontrovertible', that these laws dictate the functioning, change and 'progress' of systems of production, which among other things imposes increasing interdependence of national sub-systems on the global level. This strand of thought, however, goes much further; through the interpretation, right or wrong, of these economic realities as forces which impose themselves on history whether we want them to or not, it calls on us to submit to them. It is said that states' policies must – or should – be adjusted to the strategies of private firms and submit to their interests, which transgress national borders. This is the sense given today to the dynamic of globalisation by its champions. Optimists would say that politics and society adjust to these demands of their own accord – or do so eventually – and that this is for the best. Pessimists would say that the conflict between the economic objectivity that is imposing itself and the autonomy of politics and society (including cultural, ideological and religious aspects) can lead to societal sclerosis or, in certain cases, self-destruction.

Economic reductionism has always dominated the social thought of the right, in a form, moreover, of self-perpetuating optimism regarding the system. The resulting imperfections, or indeed social disasters, are therefore simply the product of a refusal to adjust or transitional hitches which will eventually be left behind (the word 'trickledown' perfectly expresses this forced optimism which dispenses with critical analysis of the system).

However, economic reductionism has also always had a left-wing side, and indeed there has always been an economically reductionist interpretation of Marxism itself. I would claim that the existence of this shows that, as Marx himself said, 'the ideology of the dominant class is the dominant ideology in society'. I, along with others, have related economistic alienation – the essential content of bourgeois ideology – to an objective reality: the increasing autonomy of economic law relative to the political and ideological control which was an inherent part of all previous systems. The left-wing version of economic reductionism – including vulgar Marxism – is still nevertheless reformist in the sense that it calls not for adjustment by submission to the demands of capitalist management to the unilateral profit of capital, but for the controlled framing of economic necessity (the development of productive forces) through reforms (including radical reforms modifying social relationships, singularly that of property) which would allow the progress of productive forces to be put to the service of the working classes. Today therefore, these currents tend to share with the dominant view the idea that 'globalisation is incontrovertible'. This brief overview of the attitudes of social thought regarding the challenges of the modern world also clearly invites us to enquire why responses ('what is to be done?') are so diverse, running from submission to adjustment through reform to either a revolutionary refusal (purporting to be in step with history) or a reactionary refusal (claiming the ability to turn back the clock). The objective of this chapter is not to elucidate the entire spectrum of social thought; it is much more modest than that. Initially I would situate myself on the left in that I believe neither that capitalism amounts to the end of history, nor even that it is capable of surmounting its own inherent contradictions (whose nature I will try to specify below). I will then attempt an interpretation of the problem in question within the framework of this fundamental paradigm. I will do this with the help of an interpretation of Marxism which, although I share it with others, is certainly not the only one. I will not attempt to legitimate this interpretation here. I will also consider with the utmost seriousness the contribution of thought that does not necessarily subscribe to the Marxist method, and is sometimes situated outside the Marxist problematic, as they appear to me to be decisive. I refer specifically here to the contributions of Karl Polanyi, Braudel and world-systems theory current.

Understanding historical capitalism

I will begin to discuss the questions which I have posed above by returning to the contributions of world-systems analysis. I can be brief here, having expressed myself in some detail on this subject in my article 'Capitalisme et système-monde' (Amin 1992a). I will recall here, therefore, only those of my conclusions that are essential to the following discussion.

First, capitalism is a system whose specificity by comparison with previous systems lies precisely in the dominance of economic authority. The law of value not only dictates economic life under capitalism but all aspects of social life (this is what is meant by market alienation). This qualitative reversal of the relationship between economics and politics/ideology rules out, in my opinion, the use of laws which are valid for modern history in the interpretation of pre-capitalist history. There is a historic discontinuity which rules out this sort of generalisation. Power commanded wealth, it is henceforth wealth which commands power.

Second, the capitalist system only reached its advanced form with the establishment of the mechanised factory in the 19th century (modern industry), a base which was essential to the deployment of the law of value specific to the capitalist mode of production. Given this, the three centuries which preceded this genuine Industrial Revolution constitute a transitional phase which has been accurately termed as mercantilist.

Third, the law of value must be understood at its highest level of abstraction, that of the capitalist mode of production (which implies a market integrated in all three dimensions – goods, capital and labour), and at the level of abstraction which defines the global capitalist system (which is deployed on the basis of a truncated integrated market, reduced to the first two of those dimensions). The distinction which I propose between the concept of the law of value and the globalised law of value is essential to my analysis in that only the second can explain why capitalism as a world system engenders polarisation by its very nature. The modern capitalist polarisation in question did not, therefore, appear until after the turning point of 1800 when capitalism reached its advanced form: first, as a polarisation composed of the contrast between an industrialised core and a non-industrialised periphery and then one consisting of the still developing contrast based on the 'five monopolies' (these will be discussed below under the section 'Globalisation and the continuing accumulation crisis'). Core–periphery polarisation is neither synonymous with the metropolis–colony contrast, nor particular to the stage designated as imperialism by Lenin (defined by the establishment of monopolies at the core).

Fourth, any questions related to the history of capitalism – the vicissitudes of the transitional phase of mercantilism (1500–1800), the far-off roots of its initial appearance (before 1500 in Europe and/or elsewhere), the reasons why it took root in Europe (and not elsewhere, earlier, or simultaneously elsewhere) and the phases of its expansion since 1800 – must be discussed, in my opinion, in the light of the concepts defined in the three preceding paragraphs. This methodological comment concerns as much the discussion of 'long cycles' as that of the succession of potential hegemonies and rivalries and, consequently, the inequalities (a broader term than 'polarisation' which I reserve for the effects of the globalised law of value) between countries and regions brought about by the progressive expansion of the system. To this end, I intend to examine in detail the characteristics of what I shall call the succession of phases of accumulation, emphasising the specificity of each of these phases and thus avoiding over-hasty generalisation in order to rediscover the types of general law which can be applied to the mode of repetition (the cycle in the rigorous sense of the term). This method demands that one places the debate in its true context from the start, which implies analysis of the interrelationships between the different strata proposed by Braudel (see the next section 'Separating the inseparable'), that is to say the reconstitution of the contradictory unity between economics and politics (or, in other words, the rejection of the economy vision – bourgeois or otherwise – which supposed that the economy acts alone, according to its own laws, and that politics adjusts to or reflects this). Already the globalised law of value, as distinct from the law of value, implies this contradiction of capitalism since the truncated nature of world markets (as opposed to the completed nature of national markets) integrates the political (states, strong or weak, metropolises or colonies, defined by their individual social logics) and the economic. For each of the phases of accumulation demarcated as such one must give oneself the task of defining its (or their) modes of regulation at the local (national) and global levels. The analysis of the expansion and subsequent exhaustion of these successive phases of accumulation, of the crises of their modes of regulation and the appearance of the conditions for a new phase of accumulation, should allow us to specify the exact functioning of rivalries (economic competition, political supremacies) and of potential hegemonies (a term whose ambiguity I mistrust), and consequently to understand with hindsight why and how in real history capitalism has constantly been constructed, deconstructed and reconstructed. Its flexibility is, for me, synonymous with this history. Theory is history. Theory is not the discovery of historical laws which precede history itself. This method clearly puts one on guard against the generalisation which is expressed in the proposals concerning the succession of cycles (including hegemonic cycles) which postulate an apparent regularity which cannot be attained without twisting the dynamics of real evolutions.

Fifth, the current of thought grouped under the name 'world system' does not – fortunately – propose an exclusive theory of the history of capitalism, which one must either rally to or reject completely. I share the fundamental elements of the paradigm which reunites the various theses produced within this framework: one part being the emphasis put on interdependence operating at the global level (contrary to the dominant view which regards the global system as being composed of juxtaposed national formations); the other being the emphasis put on the totalising nature of capitalism (contrary to the dominant view which stresses its economic side and subordinates its political element). Acceptance of these two pillars of this method in no way implies subscribing to a theory of cycles. The criticisms of this or more exactly these theories, prevalent among thinkers of the world-economy current, have been sufficiently developed in my article cited above (Amin, 1992a) and I will not repeat them here.

Separating the inseparable

The contribution of Braudel to our method of analysing 'historical capitalism' is well known. As we know, Braudel defines three levels of social reality: (1) at the base, the set of elementary structures which make up 'material life' on a day-to-day basis, in particular the organisation of work and subsistence within the family unit; (2) at the intermediate level, the 'market', that is to say the set of structures within which exchanges dictated by the social division of labour occur; and (3) finally, at the higher level, power; in other words, an 'anti-market' where the predators in the jungle of local and global politics stalk (Braudel 1979).

The concise nature of the formula allows us to understand immediately that Braudel rejects economic reductionism, which defines itself by its exclusive preoccupation with the intermediate level. Equally it allows us to grasp why Braudel rejects the synonym 'capitalism = market', which dominates vulgar thought, particularly the dominant contemporary fashion. For Braudel the very existence of the higher level defines the specificity of historical capitalism. According to him the market economy (the division of labour and exchanges) clearly preceded capitalism, which did not exist until the anti-market (genuine power, which history would make in its turn that of capitalism) established itself above the market. What are the conceptual tools which will enable us to try to specify both the nature of the structures which define each of these strata and the dialectic of their relationships, both conflictual and complementary? The division of academic tasks has artificially created specialisations specific to each of the strata considered. Without descending to caricature, one could say that sociologists study the base, economists the intermediate level, and political scientists and historians the upper level. We must also note that before Braudel all the great thinkers of society have tried to break down these artificial cleavages. By their very nature the dominant ideologies of the world prior to capitalism, which I have suggested calling tributary ideologies founded on metaphysical alienation which were generally religious in their expression (see Amin 1988), ignored these cleavages. Their discourses had the all-encompassing aims of explaining history and nature (through myths of creation) and formulating rules of behaviour for all levels of society, from family life to exchanges and power. Contemporary religious fundamentalism does nothing other than claim to restore this order. For my part, I would maintain that the page of metaphysical alienation has been definitively turned, precisely by the triumph of capitalism, which substitutes economic for metaphysical alienation and by the same title founds the separation of the three levels and thus the domination and autonomy of the economic. This is why I believe the year 1500 saw a qualitative transformation of the system. The philosophy of the Enlightenment, which expresses this new vision of the world, constitutes the plinth on which the subsequent autonomous 'economic science' was able to establish itself. However, the philosophy of the Enlightenment does not simply boil down to economics, but transgresses it and offers what it believes to be a science of society which reaches from the base to the summit of power. This philosophy of the Enlightenment, like the economic science whose formation it stimulated, was not accepted by all currents of social thought, even if it does still supply the essential elements of dominant theory. The work of Marx, starting with the discovery and denunciation of market alienation (and thus the refusal to consider capitalism as the end of history), constructed a historical materialism whose very name implies the preoccupation with transgressing the economic and re-establishing the unity of the three levels subsequently described by Braudel.

Marx

This observation will allow us to situate each of the books of *Capital* in the construction of this project. Volume I essentially concerns the base – and market alienation – but does not place it outside the fundamental relations of production which define capitalism. On the contrary, it places it at the heart of the relationship of exploitation of labour by capital (and of the destruction of nature by capital, an aspect little understood by readers of Marx and even less others). Volume II then proposes from this base an analysis of the economics of the system, or the economics of the capitalist mode of production (the law of value), at its highest level of abstraction. The dynamics of the balance of productions of the two departments which produce material elements ensuring the domination of labour by capital and the elements of material consumption which allow the reproduction of the labour force, are the very essence of Volume II. However, Marx's project did not stop there. Over and above this economic analysis, which one could term as pure (proposed in opposition to the other 'pure economics', namely classical economics based on the philosophy of the Enlightenment and, later, in response to Marx's project, neoclassical economics, justly designated as vulgar as it does not question economic alienation), Marx elevated his analysis to the higher level (as Braudel defines it) by the construction of an analytical framework of power and the global system. Marx's project remained incomplete and is undoubtedly imperfect, as are all human endeavours. I will summarise my observations on these themes in the following four points.

First, in Volume I of *Capital* the exclusive preoccupation with discovering the roots of capitalist exploitation leads Marx to separate the system of exchange (of goods but also of the sale of labour power) from that which is apparently situated outside it: the system of satisfaction of needs through subsistence and especially through the organisation of the family. The latter discovery was rightly questioned by the feminist discovery of the limitations of Marx, a man of the 19th century. Nevertheless, historical Marxism has not been as royally uninterested in the elementary level of social construction as is sometimes claimed. Volume I does not have to be read in ignorance of the philosophical writings of Marx (which stress alienation) and of other Marxists (who have sometimes tried to extend the project in order to integrate psychological science into the ensemble of social construction), or in ignorance of writings which deal directly with the family and male–female relationships. Whatever one may think of the conclusions drawn by Engels at the time (that the origins of the family were linked precisely with those of private property and the state), this initiative opened the way for a Marxist anthropology which subsequently yielded results which, albeit uncertain and partial, were certainly important. I would therefore say that it is still possible for the elementary level in question to be better integrated in the historical materialist framework. I would even contend that the efforts of conventional sociology (including Weber) have yielded even more uncertain and partial results, as is only to be expected given that anti-Marxist prejudices have led them to try and analyse this level in neglect of its relationship to economics and power. However, I would no more contend that we possess a body of established theses based on the method of historical materialism that would allow us either to be satisfied or to conclude that historical materialism is already outdated; much more groundwork must be done before we have explored its potential capabilities.

Second, the relationships between society and nature were not ignored by Marx. However, they were not treated sufficiently systematically but only in passing, notably in *Capital*, Book I, Chapter XV, last sentence of Section X (where there are many allusions and references to the destruction of the natural base on which the expansion of capital is founded) and in the writings of other

Marxists. Here even more must be done, stimulated as we must be by the ecological challenge, even if up to now the contribution of analyses developed by this current remains small. But we must also recognise that historical Marxism has, in fact, largely ignored this particular problematic.

Third, the relationships concerning power, and therefore the integration of the higher level, as Braudel defines it, to the ensemble of the construction are, in my opinion, the area least understood. I refer the reader here to my book *Eurocentrism* (1988). Granted, some important work has been done in this field and neither the work of Marx and Engels (in their political writings), nor that of the Marxists (notably in the theories of imperialism of Lenin, Bukharin and others), nor that of Braudel (concerning the mercantilist tradition) should be ignored. However, in my opinion, fundamental questions, those which I have termed as questions relative to the alienations inherent to power, remain unanswered to this day. Even in studies of the modern age of capitalism (from the mercantilist transition through to advanced capitalism) questions about the interrelationship between political and economic and financial power are the least thoroughly discussed. There are, of course, some major theories on the subject. Anti-Marxist theories generally start from the hypothesis of quasi-independent or even supreme political authority (a necessary appendage of economic reductionism). I will not discuss these theories here. Other theses, Marxist and otherwise, have reduced politics to the mere reflection of economic exigencies. The thesis that the state and the economy are dominated by capital at the monopoly stage of capitalism belongs in this category. Of course, variants have been much affected by the specificities of their countries of origin – the opposition between the German form developed by Hilferding and the British form developed by Hobson is well known – but this has not always prevented abusive generalisations (to which Lenin was no stranger). Other theses deal more specifically with the political power–'high finance' relationship of the mercantilist period. The works of Braudel and those whom he has inspired in the world-economy school (notably Arrighi 1994) are also very important. I will return to the debates surrounding the relationship between the dominant capitalist economic power and the 'territorialist' dimension of capitalism (political expansion) because they are essential to an understanding of our central subject, the nature of the global system. I remain wary, however, of the universalising theories advanced by some – such as the Leninist theory of imperialism or the profoundly non-territorialist thesis of capitalist hegemonies inspiring Braudel and Arrighi – as I believe that their account of the political–economic relationship remains shaky.

Fourth, the major weakness of Marx's project, and of subsequent historical Marxism, concerns the relationship between the capitalist mode of production and capitalist globalisation. This weakness is clearly relevant to our subject and is also the most pressing of the challenges confronting the societies of the modern world. It is therefore the major political question. The thesis which I have developed on this subject (see Amin, 1994a) is that Marx himself and then, especially, historical Marxism conceived of globalisation to a great extent as simply the worldwide expansion of the capitalist mode of production. The perspective of progressive homogenisation of the world which this reduction implies would completely exclude a correct assessment of the factors behind the polarisation caused by the worldwide expansion of capitalism. This vision was only partially corrected by Lenin, whose thesis of revolution starting in the periphery and spreading to the centre testifies to the same error. The core–periphery contrast was consequently never subjected to sufficient theoretical examination and is thus confused with or reduced to, for instance, the metropolis–colony contrast. This weakness of historical Marxism could only engender tragic consequences, of which the blind alley taken by the Russian Revolution was not the least. Indeed, historical Marxism shares this major blunder with all political currents of the left – social democratic and radical democratic – and, at this level, rejoins vulgar bourgeois thought, which is incapable of treating inequality as anything other than a manifestation of backwardness. My conclusion is therefore that historical Marxism and the left in general are poorly equipped to face the challenge of globalisation. It is their Achilles' heel and, as we shall see, the heart of the challenge which confronts modern societies.

Historical materialism and the 'world seen as market'

Certain important contributions, extending the tools of analysis produced by Marxism, have perhaps corrected or at least begun to correct the deficiencies of historical Marxism identified here. If I attach most importance to the contribution of Karl Polanyi (1944[1994]) in this field it is because it is among the few attempts to recognise the global dimension of capitalism. Polanyi's thesis is, as we know, based on a rejection of the idea that the market can be self-regulating. On this basis he attacks the very foundations of bourgeois economism, which today blows its trumpet louder than ever. Polanyi shows that the commodification of the labour force, of nature and of money can only create chaos and intolerable social deprivation. The utopia pursued by capital whenever political circumstances allow has thus never lasted long. Here I refer the reader to my writings on the subject in *La Gestion capitalists de la crise* (Amin 1995).

The three themes addressed by Polanyi can be found in Marx; most notable is the alienation of labour, to which I shall not return. However, on the theme of nature, Polanyi makes explicit what was not developed systematically enough by Marx (and still less so by historical Marxism). The question of money was, on the other hand, the subject of long discussions in *Capital*, Volume III, regarding credit, crises and international exchanges; in the course of these analyses Marx proposed a problematic of the money–power relationship and a reflection on monetary fetishism.

Marx developed this last theme in great detail. He demonstrated how the cycle of money (M) could apparently 'liberate' itself from the path dictated by production (P) through contrasting the productive cycle of M-P-M' (in which money-capital is immobilised in the equipment necessary for capitalist production, in other words in the means of exploiting labour which creates the greatest surplus value (M')), with the money-usurer/rentier cycle of M-M' which is the supreme expression of monetary fetishism. We will return later to this point which I regard as essential to the nature of the contemporary crisis and its management. On the money–power relationship Marx also supplies the conceptual equipment which shows how money – the symbol of purchasing power – became the symbol of power, plain and simple. Money cannot therefore be treated as any other product, as vulgar economic reductionism in its most wretched manifestations – such as those currently dominant (the so-called monetarist school or liberalism, whatever that means, etc) – would have us believe. I have therefore already tried to propose an analysis of the money–power relationship which highlights the necessary management of money and credit by the state, acting here as the capitalist collective overcoming the conflicts at market level. Within this framework, I describe the functions of this management in the competitive regulation in the 19th century, the monopolistic and Fordist regulation of the 20th century and regulation considered on a global scale (see Amin 1994a, especially Chapter 8).

What Polanyi offers us here is an authoritative account of the development of liberal utopianism from the end of the 19th century to the final catastrophe which it engendered – Fascism and the Second World War. He does this by linking the national dimensions of the destructive (and not self-regulating) functioning of labour, land and money markets with their global dimension. In depicting the battle lines of the positions taken up by societies following the disaster, Polanyi gives us the means to understand how the miraculous period of post-war growth could occur; the limits imposed on the commodification of labour by the historic social democratic compromise between labour and capital; and control of money by the state at national level and at the international level by the Bretton Woods institutions. My own interpretation of this post-war period (which has now run its course), which develops the beginnings made by Polanyi 40 years ago on the eve of economic take-off, is based on what I have called the three pillars of the global system (the historic social-democratic compromise, Sovietism and the bourgeois nationalist project of Bandung). This interpretation owes much to the method proposed by Polanyi. Certainly the success of this post-war model had its limits at both the national and the global level. Among other things nothing was done to limit the ravages of the commodification of nature, despite the alarm bells sounded by Polanyi. It is therefore no accident that the question of the environment has exploded like a time-bomb towards the end of this period. We should have expected it.

This post-war phase of expansion is now over, following the

collapse of the three pillars which supported it. The rapid come-back of liberal utopianism (the triple commodification in question operates freely at the global level, the self-regulating nature attributed to the market being used to justify these policies) should not surprise us. However, it is not capable in itself of defining a new phase of capitalist expansion and is in fact merely crisis management (see the title of my 1995 book). Unfortunately, as I have said, the left and historical Marxism are poorly equipped to take up the challenge. Even more than during the post-war period the sclerosis of dogmatic Marxism has deprived us of the means truly to understand the mechanisms, the contradictions and the limitations of the three models considered (social-democratic, Soviet and Third World nationalist), and so serious analysis has been replaced by a simplified and weighted ideological discourse.

I return now to Braudel, whose contribution regarding what we have recalled of Marxism can perhaps be appreciated.

Reading Braudel's magnificent work is certainly always a pleasure, and I know of little writing which is as enjoyable as that concerning 'material life', that is to say his precise description of the founding strata of society. It is true, however, that Braudel's generous presentation fails to link up the systems of material life with those that command the higher levels of social construction, perhaps because, anxious to avoid the Marxist temptation, Braudel chose to ignore the concepts of the relations of reproduction and the theory of alienation. In Braudel's favour we should note that his work is on the mercantilist period, that is the period prior to the relations of exploitation specific to advanced capitalism.

Analysis of characteristics particular to the intermediate stratum – that of exchange – also contributes more, I think, to an understanding of the mercantilist period to which Braudel dedicated his work than to that of industrial capitalism. Analysis of this system as one of exchange is sufficient to the extent that mercantile capital and the exploitation of both artisan and craft manufacturing are dominant, as they were for the period 1500–1800 (or 1350–1800). However, I am still of the opinion that this analysis is insufficient for what was to follow. This is not only because the field of exchange assumed a size unknown before the Industrial Revolution in 1800 (previous exchanges could only affect a limited fraction of either the labour force or production), but more because it was henceforth to be dominated by industrial rather than mercantile capital. It is therefore no accident that Braudel ignores the law of value, a weakness unfortunately later perpetuated by many authors of the world-system school (indeed, Arrighi 1994, ignores both the law of value in general and the globalised law of value in this superb work). Nor is it by accident that these authors systematically devalue the concept of Industrial Revolution. The matter in question here is not, in my opinion, whether or not this revolution was as rapid as is sometimes said, or whether it was set in motion by the interaction of 'internal factors', or whether the asymmetry defined by the positions of the core–periphery contrast peculiar to the mercantilist stage was the decisive factor in the change (these debates have for me their own value and interest). The question we must ask is quite simply whether the new industries represented a qualitative jump in the underlying organisation of the system. Convinced as I am that this was in fact the case, I would draw two conclusions from my central opinions. The first is that the core–periphery system particular to advanced capitalism is different by its very nature from that which characterised the mercantilist transition. The second is that to view the intermediate level after 1800 as a system of exchange inevitably flattens, impoverishes and reduces analysis to the point where, whether one likes it or not, it becomes equivalent to the conventional bourgeois vision of 'the world seen as a market'.

Braudel's major contribution to the understanding of capitalism comes therefore in the emphasis that he puts on the third level of reality: 'the anti-market' whose very existence is denied by the dominant economically reductionist school of social thought which disregards its decisive nature in the true definition of capitalism. Clearly no reasoning person can deny that the state and politics exist. However, the world seen as a market would imply a conception of the state radically different from that with which real history presents us. I have made an inroad into the field by taking up the thesis of Walras, the purest of the economic reductionists, and taking at face-value the aspiration to build a world that is a market (see Amin 1995). Walras demonstrates that the market cannot act as a self-regulating force giving optimal results unless private property is rescinded under a system that puts capital up for auction. This 'capitalism without capitalists' perspective was, in my interpretation of Soviet history, the guiding principle of the strategy that was incorrectly termed as socialist construction. In this perspective, global socialism would therefore be a global market fully integrated in all its dimensions: the present states would be abolished and replaced by a global state which would run this perfect market. Clearly this vision and programme are not only utopian in the vulgar sense of the word but also completely ignore both reality and the theory of alienation. Neither Marx nor Braudel conceived of the economy–power relationship in this way.

We can thus return to Braudel (1979) who gives us a brilliant explanation of the birth of capitalist power, not as the spontaneous product of the market but, on the contrary, as something outside and above market-imposed constraints. Braudel terms the qualitative transformation which became apparent in Europe at the end of the Middle Ages as the passage from fragmented and decaying power to a concentrated power of which, first, the Italian towns, then the United Provinces in the 17th century, and then England from 1688 onwards, were the successive models. It is this transformation which signals the appearance of, and defines, capitalism, rather than the existence of trading, which had existed long before these developments. As we can see, Braudel's thesis concurs with mine at this point (Amin 1988); effectively I would class the specificity of the European feudal system as an example of this fragmented power, in contrast with the concentrated power in tributary systems elsewhere (in China for example). I would define this difference as that between peripheral and central forms of the tributary mode. In this contrast can be found the reasons for the success of the rapid transition to capitalism in Europe (a peripheral tributary system), as opposed to the constant faltering of comparable developments elsewhere (in central tributary systems). In Europe the concentration of power effectively coincided with the acquisition by that power of a capitalist content whereas the concentration had already existed elsewhere. There is no comparable counterpart elsewhere to the Italian towns and the United Provinces, governed by genuine administrative councils dominated by their major capitalists, and later to the mercantilist states (in particular England and France).

The formation and triumph of capitalism is therefore the product not of a linear evolutionary expansion of markets but of an interaction between this evolution and internal factors specific to the peripheral form of the tributary mode in Europe. In this way, then, the mercantilist transition (1500–1800) can clearly be seen as a transition to advanced capitalism and thus merits in its turn the designation capitalist. I join here the view of the world system current which terms all modern history from 1500 onwards as capitalist. Subscribing to this view does not imply neglecting the importance of the qualitative transformation which came with modern industry from 1800 onwards.

Globalisation: a historicised perspective

The discussion of the available conceptual tools in the preceding section should help us to clarify the central questions: what is globalisation; what are the stakes; what challenges does its existence present to our societies? It should at least help us to differentiate between (relatively) established theses on the subject on the one hand and, on the other hand, those questions which remain outstanding with no convincing answer in so far as only conflicting hypotheses are available. (What is meant here is simple hypotheses as opposed to theses with a satisfactory paradigmatic and conceptual basis within which to situate facts.)

The term globalisation has, as is often the case in the social sciences, many very different accepted usages. According to the various points of view, we could take globalisation to mean the establishment of a global market for goods and capital, the universal character of competing technologies, the progression towards a global system of production, the political weight that the global system carries in the competition for global or regional hegemonies, the cultural aspect of universalisation, etc. There are thus broader or narrower definitions which are more or less rigorous. Given this fact, theories concerning the more or less constraining nature of globalisation, its stability or instability, its progression (continuous or jerky) and the potential phases of which it is constituted, vary according to the conceptual definitions employed.

Deregulation, which is in itself a deliberate policy which must be consciously undertaken rather than a natural state of affairs which imposes itself, releases the strategies of large enterprise from the constraints which states' policies can otherwise represent. However, the facts show that these independent strategies of private firms do not form a coherent ensemble guaranteeing the stability of a new order. On the contrary, they create chaos and by their very nature reveal the vulnerability of the globalisation process, which may be thrown into doubt in consequence.

In its broadest sense globalisation refers to the existence of relations between the different regions of the world and, as a corollary, the reciprocal influence that societies exert upon one another. Using this sense of the term I have proposed a descriptive schema of the ancient world system, that of the tributary age – from 500 to 300 BC to AD 1500 – relating the three major core tributary systems of these two millennia (China, India and the Middle East) to the peripheries (Europe, Africa, South-East Asia, Korea and Japan) through definitions of the specific concepts of the cores and the peripheries peculiar to this pre-capitalist past. These concepts are defined in the dominant sphere of the organisation of power rather than in the economic sphere as is the case for capitalism (we thus avoid the use of concepts specific to capitalism in the analysis of the pre-capitalist era, a use which is unfortunately common among certain world-system theorists). My analysis of this ancient system (Amin 1991, 1992a) leads me to a conclusion which is important to note here: the ancient system was not by nature polarising but, on the contrary, favoured catch up (historical delays): for example, Europe hoisted itself in a brief historical period from a peripheral position to that of the new centre (through the transformation from feudalism to absolute monarchy) in the course of the transition to capitalism, thus becoming the core (in the singular) on the global scale for the first time in history.

Arrighi (1994) illustrates the non-polarising nature of the ancient system in his analysis of the apparently curious behaviour of the Ming Dynasty of China which, although perfectly capable of achieving maritime pre-eminence, did not do so. China was more advanced than Europe and there was thus nothing the Chinese wished to buy in the west, so they did not apply themselves to controlling the westward maritime routes. China thus allowed the Europeans – Portuguese and Dutch, and then English and French – to establish their dominance of the maritime route to the east (from their own perspective), a fact which would help the Europeans to overcome their backwardness. The new mercantilist world system built itself on the ruins of the old system which it progressively destroyed, reorganising the flux of exchanges to the benefit of the European core. In this sense the year 1500 clearly represents a major historical turning point. With hindsight the mercantilist period (1500–1800) thus seems to be a moment of transition to capitalism, if one defines capitalism's advanced form as stemming from the emergence of modern industry, when industrial capital imposed its logic of accumulation on existing mercantile capital. Of course, if this occurred, it was because of the specific way in which the forms of globalisation put in place by mercantilism interacted with internal facets of the transformation particular to Europe (which I have suggested analysing as a bourgeois hegemony operating in the context of absolute monarchy as the organising principle of power), which were different from those of the major tributary hegemonies. In this way 1800 also signals a major historical turning point. In sharp contrast with the tributary world system, non-polarising by nature, the mercantilist system was based on a previously unknown polarisation. This polarisation would assume its full magnitude in its turn following 1800, in the framework of the advanced capitalist world system. In 1800, as Paul Bairoch (1994) has established, the differences between levels of development in the principal large regions of the world were still relatively minor. The gaps became much wider in the next 150 years (1800–1950) in the framework of the new capitalist polarisation, in which the core–periphery opposition corresponded almost exactly with that between the industrialised countries and those whose industrial revolution had yet to begin, a process which was already coming to look impossibly difficult. This new and, as history has proved, polarising globalisation can clearly not be explained by a simple schema equally valid for the period in its entirety and for all the regions concerned. The diverse functions of the different peripheries (always to be referred to in the plural), the dialectic between exterior constraints and internal responses, the strategies particular to the different competing metropolises, the phases of capitalist development in the core (notably the transition from competition to oligopolies around 1880), the evolution of the regulatory systems of accumulation (regulation of competition, the historic compromise between labour and capital, Keynesian management, etc) in both the core and on the global scale: all these factors invite us to distinguish distinct phases of the 1800–1950 period and core–periphery models presenting significant particularities. However, above all, these specificities of the law of accumulation on the global scale – which I believe is most usefully conceptualised in terms of a globalised law of value specifying the functioning of the law of value at the level of the global system would inevitably engender polarisation by its inherent dynamic. I have attributed the polarising character of this law to the fact that it operates in a two-dimensional market (a market of goods and capital tending to integration on the global level), truncated in comparison with markets integrated in three dimensions (where the labour market is also integrated) which are particular to the national bourgeois constructions and are the foundation of the law of value. I will not return here to this central point in my analysis. In the following four sub-sections I will address questions other than those related to post-Second World War globalisation and to contemporary perspectives. I will touch upon questions related to the interpretation of modern (mercantilist and industrial) globalisation: questions related to cycles, hegemonies, the potential territorialism associated with capitalist expansion, and the financialisation of capital.

Cycles and phases

I have expressed my point of view regarding the question of cycles elsewhere (Amin 1994a) in sufficient detail and I will not return to it here. There are in history dates which constitute major turning points (in my own view, 1500 and 1800); between these turning points there are undoubtedly other dates which allow us to identify particular sub-phases (1880 and 1920 for instance, also 1945 or 1950 and 1980 or 1990, although these are perhaps of a different stature from the major breaks). However this does not imply any concession to a long-cycle theory. It neither implies a quest to mark out 'recurrences' which transcend each of the major phases defined, nor proposes a philosophy of history where repetition – albeit on an ascending trend – assumes more importance than the identification of qualitative transformation. Projection onto the past – for example, projection of what is new about industrial capitalism (the inherent tendency to overproduction and the crises in which this is manifested) onto the previous mercantilist period, or of what is new in capitalism (the hegemony of the market and economic reductionism) onto previous periods (the tributary system, commanded by other organising principles of the power–economy relationship) – has always appeared to me to be an error which serves to conceal real history. It is not essential to the concept of a world system. Instead of these cycle theory propositions, I believe it is more productive to centre the objective of analysis on the identification of phases of accumulation. This allows us both to respect the specificities of each phase (avoiding confusing mercantile relations with relationships particular to industrial capitalism, etc) and to link the economics of each phase with its politics (the mode of operation of power, hegemonic social blocs, etc). We will return to this essential relationship.

Hegemonies

I will not, however, discuss any further the question of hegemonies and the theory of successive hegemonies (the Italian cities, the Netherlands, Great Britain, the United States) advanced by some, I still have many reservations regarding the methodology which guides these theories.

Hegemony appears to me to be the exception rather than the rule in the course of history. To speak of the hegemony of the Italian cities or the Netherlands, however precocious the societies in question might have been, is to employ the term in a vague manner which ignores the realities dictating the insertion of these countries into the systems (regional and, partially, global) of the time. Even British hegemony, which I would not situate before the Industrial Revolution, only imposed itself because of the exceptional conjunction of a monopoly of the new industrial technology (eroded from the second half of the 19th century onwards), the financial power of London (which existed until 1945) and an enormous colonial empire – perhaps the only one worthy of the name – which grouped together both colonies of exploitation (India) and colonies which were populated both before and after the period in question (not least of them the future United

States, which subsequently assured the global domination of the English language). However, despite the phenomenal nature of this hegemony, it too had considerable limits. It prevailed only partially over the independent American continent, over China, Japan and the Ottoman empire, etc. Lacking a military hegemony (apart from naval predominance), Great Britain was forced to forge a balance of power among the strong nations of Europe (Germany, France, Russia), thus limiting, among other things, English cultural hegemony (which did not become predominant until disseminated by the United States) and English political hegemony – a fact which made Britain incapable of resisting the rise of competing imperial powers (Germany, Japan, the United States, France).

The British model of hegemony has nonetheless inspired competitors, notably in the colonial sphere (where only France, the Netherlands and Belgium achieved any results, and even these were comparatively very modest). Others, such as Germany, were not able to imitate Britain, or were provided with an alternative (continental expansion for the United States and Russia). Furthermore, in two decisive fields – industrial competitiveness and military power – Great Britain was rapidly out-distanced by its rivals. Nevertheless, it long retained a financial advantage whose importance we shall return to later in this chapter.

The hegemony of the United States after the Second World War derived from a different conjunction of factors of power. In this case the formidable industrial advance proved to be the result of passing circumstances (the state of the world in 1945) and was rapidly eroded by the European and Japanese recoveries. But, as with Great Britain, the financial advantage appears able to continue despite the relative decline of industrial competitiveness. Also, if the US has not broken with its so-called anti-colonial tradition (i.e. its weak propensity for colonial conquest), it is simply because its absolute and unprecedented military power, limited only temporarily (from 1945 to 1990) by the only other superpower of this order (now in tatters), freed it from the need for colonial conquest. It is also because of its unprecedented influence that the US has made the English language what it is today, something it could not have been in the 19th century.

Territorialism

What has sometimes been referred to as 'territorialism', that is to say the propensity to extend the area controlled by a single political centre, maintains an extremely complicated relationship with capitalist expansion. The question also intersects in a more general manner with the political–economic relationship particular to capitalism. Two extreme positions on the question of territorialism appear to me sterile.

The first position sees capitalism as a system which is by nature territorially disembodied. However elegant this definition might be – and it still implies exterior economic relations in the framework of the state (large or small) which have important effects on the interior, to a degree never seen in previous ages – it remains essentially misleading. In fact, existing capitalism has guided the spatial relationship between its economic reproduction and its area of political control in a way that cannot be understood if the question of territorialism is excluded. The Italian cities, certainly, had influence far beyond their frontiers and the United Provinces constituted a relatively large small country. Modern states of diverse size still exist and the small ones are not necessarily less successful than the large in terms of their global insertion. Indeed certain micro-states (Luxembourg, Liechtenstein, the Bahamas, the oil-producing emirates) have found profitable loopholes for this insertion. The US and Russia are continent-states without exterior colonies (the Russian empire and the Soviet Union are multinational and not colonial). However, conversely, the global position of Great Britain cannot be understood without its colonial empire, nor can that of France between 1880 and 1960 (since then France has chosen to operate its insertion through European integration and no longer through its neocolonial zone of influence). Why these differences?

This variety of situations – in both space and time – thus rules out the equation: cores/peripheries = metropolises/colonies. Unfortunately this equation is popular and has partly become so through an excessive simplification of the theses of Hobson, Hilferding and Lenin concerning modern imperialism.

The fashion today is to disregard all these specificities, which are nonetheless major in my opinion. Thus the term 'empire' is used, incorrectly and to cross-purposes, to mix pell-mell the Roman empire, the Byzantine, the Caliphates and the Ottoman, the Chinese, the Austro-Hungarian, the Russian, the British and the French. But these formations are totally different not only in their internal structure but also in their mode of insertion into globalisation. Oppression, racist, ethnic, cultural or national oppression, is not a new phenomenon. However, capitalist exploitation and core–periphery polarisation, its potential colonial form, are realities particular to the modern age and specific forms of insertion into globalisation. Again, although the Russian empire (then the Soviet Union) might well have been a prison for its people, it was not a colonial empire organised in the same way as that of Britain. In the Soviet empire economic transfers were made from the Russian core to the Asiatic peripheries, in direct opposition to the situation in the British empire (see Amin 1994b).

The relationship of territorialism to capitalism brings us to the question of power in capitalism. The simplistic thesis that power is based on capital and nothing else may contain a useful nugget of truth but does not cast much light on the variety of situations that can emerge. I return here to what I said above (under the subsection 'Separating the inseparable') on Braudel's description of the three levels of capitalist reality. Capitalism is not the market but 'the market + the anti-market which expresses itself in the actions of political power'. The power of high finance (which is in fact a merchant–artisan–financier coalition in the mercantilist stage) supplies the foundation for the construction of the first capitalist states: the Italian towns and the United Provinces. Here Arrighi usefully draws attention to the fact that no power has been so close to the extreme model of a state governed by an administrative council of large firms as these modest political formations. However, the crystallisation of the political power/economic space association capable of achieving the qualitative jump that industrialisation represented for the capitalist mode of production did not occur here. It occurred in the great mercantilist states' mutation – England first and then France – into modern bourgeois states with autocentred (though not isolationist) economies and thus in the identity between the area of accumulation and its political management. This model was reproduced in Germany and elsewhere, because it genuinely responded to the demands of the capitalism of the time. These fundamental requirements with colonies (England, France) or without (Germany), more or less assured similar results in terms of the construction of economic competitiveness on the global scale. This model thus became the subject of a powerful ideologisation, establishing the equation between its completion and that of progress and modernity. Of course, it is impossible to grasp the efficacy of this history without the use of analysis and a theory of the social hegemonies on which the power of capital was founded, the social alliances (with the aristocracy, then the peasantry, later the social compromise of capital and labour, etc) which permitted them, and so on. Marx made this thorough analysis for his own age. Marxists of high calibre – Gramsci among others – have continued his work.

Colonial or semi-colonial expansion grafted itself onto this history. It can thus perhaps be seen as an appendage of the social hegemonies specific to such countries in the relevant phase of their capitalist development, Examples might include the connections between the expansion of the English cotton industry and the destruction of that of India; between industrial specialisation in England and growing argicultural imports from the US and the largely uninhabited territories; as well as between the mediocrity of certain sectors of French agriculture and industry and the existence of reserved colonial markets (as is shown by the work of Marseille, 1984). It can thus be seen that colonies are not an absolute prerequisite for the expansion of capital but merely for certain types of social hegemony in this expansion.

The propensity towards colonial expansion nevertheless appears to become practically generalised from 1880 onwards (colonial empires extant at this date had been largely inherited from mercantilist constructions previous to 1800 – India, Indonesia, etc). This was not the result of an absolute requirement of internal accumulation, as rapid and superficial analyses have often claimed, but the result of sharpened competition between the new oligopolies even if, clearly, the dominant national capital knew how to profit from colonisation. Lenin never claimed otherwise, even if he has subsequently been interpreted as doing so. The success – or the failure – of this colonial expansion has furthermore had complex effects, positive and negative, regarding accumulation itself, sometimes putting the pillaged resources of over-exploitation at its disposal, sometimes, on the other hand, retarding the development of backward productive sectors. Portugal and the Netherlands are the classic examples of these negative effects. However, for France and even for England, which initially exploited the colonisation of India so effectively, these negative effects were not completely absent in the subsequent evolution of globalised competition. Other factors of success or failure – more even than the national mastery of technological progress – such as control of the process of financialisation, to which I will return, certainly do not seem to me to have been any less important.

Territorialism in the mercantilist transition can only be analysed by the same method on condition that the difference between the hegemony of mercantile capital (merchant-financier) of 1500–1800 and that of industrial capital (industrialist-financier) from 1800 onwards is fully understood. I will not develop this theme here, but in the next subsection will propose certain reflections on the subject, analysed from the particular angle of the financialisation of mercantilism.

The second position, just as sterile, if not more so, sees nothing new in capitalism (whether mercantilist or industrial) and analyses the political-economic relationship in the same terms for both ancient and modern times.

The theory of the reversal of political dominance over economics in tributary systems, to that of economic dominance over politics under capitalism (which I have proposed elsewhere (Amin 1988)), makes it impossible to treat the relationship between the space of political management and the reproduction of economic life (the concept of accumulation has no meaning in periods prior to capitalism) in the same way throughout history.

In tributary systems, economic life remains compartmentalised, even when the trade, including long-distance commerce, exerts important effects on society. The political space, on the other hand, tends to be larger in advanced tributary systems (the model being China), while it remains compartmentalised just as economic life is in the most primitive peripheral models (the European High Middle Ages) and is at a level between these two extremes in intermediate cases (the Middle East and the Islamic world, Europe at the end of the Middle Ages, India).

Financialisation of capital

What can be called the financialisation of the system (modern, capitalist) is a process by which financial capital affirms its dominance over productive capital: in the terms proposed by Marx, the dominance of the direct process M-M' (converting money into money) over the productive process M-P-M'.

Certainly, like many other phenomena, this process repeats itself in the history of capitalism, to the extent that Arrighi interprets it not as the final phase of capitalism (as is suggested by the 'highest stage of imperialism' theses of Hobson, Hilferding and Lenin) but as a recurring phenomenon. It remains to be seen if the recurrence is regular or cyclic, and whether it is useful to emphasise this factor by overlooking the specificities of financialisation at different stages of capitalist development.

I prefer to highlight these specificities. For example, the productive process M-P-M' analysed by Marx is specific to advanced industrial capitalism. P supposes the purchase of labour power and its exploitation in forms of formal submission to capital (incarnated in privately appropriated means of industrial production). In the mercantilist transition the major process of accumulation follows the formula M-E-M' where E expresses the domination of the trading exchange – buying and selling goods. Of course the products exchanged must themselves first be produced. However, they are produced by peasant and artisanal means of production which are dominated by their real and non-formal (in the sense that Marx gave to the two terms) submission to commercial capital. I would claim that this qualitative difference gives a different content to financialisation in the mercantilist period as compared to that in industrial capitalism.

In his excellent book Arrighi (1994) offers us a striking tableau of cycles in what he considers to have been the centres of the system at different times (the Italian cities of Florence, Venice, Milan and Genoa; the United Provinces), moving from supremacy through financialisation and into decline. It remains important, however, to historicise the nature of the competitiveness in question in each instance. This can be done with some ease at the level of production in certain cases, for instance in cottage industries and textile manufacture in Florence or ship-building in the United

Provinces, However, the dominant form of hegemony – coherent with the nature of mercantilism – is commercial superiority, which is, in its turn, the result of a number of factors: knowledge and control of routes (including military control); efficacy of the system of payments (the letter of change which makes the transport of cash unnecessary); superiority of means of transport (fleets); and attractive prices. On this last point Wallerstein (1974) has shown how exploitation of American mines shook up commercial flows in favour of the Europeans, who were able to offer better prices than all their competitors in the ancient tributary world system. Through all these means mercantilism effectively destroyed the ancient tributary world system (non-polarising by nature) and substituted a mercantilist world system based on polarisation; this paved the way for an advanced capitalist world system which is polarising by nature.

The financialisation of a segment of the mercantilist system is linked, then, with the establishment of adequate productive systems, the foundation for the expansion of capital at each stage. Arrighi offers us the magnificently clear example of the financialisation of Genoa following the conquest and exploitation of America. Genoa, having become the banker of the Spanish monarchy, clearly gained much more from its involvement in this evolution than it would have had it remained a simple commercial town. In the same manner Florence evolved from a town of craftsmen and merchants to become the banker of the developing absolutist European states it financialised itself. The United Provinces, originally a country of carriers and merchants, became rich by capturing much of the finance capital available in Europe and the rest of the world, and becoming in its turn the banker of Europe.

However, as always, financialisation only enriches some to the detriment of others; only the progress of production provides a way out of this zero-sum game. Thus the process M-M' is always a factor in the intensification of the inequality of incomes in favour of the dominant rentier-usurers. The process exhausts itself if it does not in part constitute a growing productive base. If the productive base does genuinely establish itself outside the financialised centre, a need is implied for effective political domination of large territories. Territorialism is associated here with competition from new, rising centres, driving the old financialised centres

95

into decline. Historically, the productive sphere has expanded on two different bases: one is exemplified in the exploitation of the Americas (mining production and the establishment of plantations – notably sugar); the other resulted from the spatial constitution of the large absolutist monarchies (which spawned the great manufacturers, the ancestors of industry). The highest performers have been those of states which politically dominated both their 'national' territories, colonies (America, then later India and Indonesia) and the trade networks, allowing them to transfer to their profit the surplus from products in which they dominated the market. However, there has never been a simple fatality operating in this framework and the advantage of rapid financialisation became a handicap, especially if political cohesion (produced by an adequate social hegemony, implying that the mechanisms of internal factors must be articulated with the mechanisms of globalisation) or military power were lacking. This is why Spain – which possessed America – never managed to keep the profit of its exploitation. The United Provinces, having reached the summit of its financial wealth, also entered into decline, having failed to create a sufficiently large mercantile territory. Their exterior concentration on their colonies was, as we know, associated with a decline in their position in Europe. There were two major successes. The first was England, which was non-financialised at the time and whose colonial empire came much later and did not assume major importance until the conquest of India in the 18th century. Second, but far behind, came France. It is this productive mercantilism which paved the way for the Industrial Revolution.

Arrighi's superb concrete analysis of the history of mercantilism illustrates the functioning of the interrelationship between financialisation and territorialism in the creation of conditions for the progress of the forces of production. The financialisation of the Netherlands did not create an effective springboard for progress there. Despite its role as the banker of the dynastic coalitions which liquidated the medieval system and created the modern interstate system (which can be dated from the Treaty of Westphalia in 1648), Holland could never control the system which it had contributed to creating. It fell to England and France to do so through the invention of mercantilism, that is at once economic nationalism (Colbertism, the Navigation Act), colonial slavery and settlers' colonies. They needed sufficient territorial space to do this. Must countries playing the role of rentier-financier always become victims of their artificial and vulnerable wealth, and be defeated by other more productive, active and inventive centres? We shall address this question to more recent times below.

Despite appearances, the history of financialisation does not repeat itself. The new industrial world system – with its unprecedented polarisation between industrialised cores and non-industrialised peripheries – was constructed in the 19th century under the auspices of Great Britain, combining, as I have remarked, technological initiative, commercial dominance, colonial exploitation, and control of the new world financial system. The ideology of free trade on which British hegemony was founded in fact brings together the cosmopolitanism of transnational capitalism and an imperial territorialism without equal. Great Britain rapidly lost its certain technological advantage over Germany and the US from the 1880s onwards. However, it kept the financial advantage until 1945. From this date on the US wrested the monopoly from its competitor through the Bretton Woods institutions. Great Britain, largely financialised from the end of the 19th century, remains 'rich' from this fact, despite its relative industrial decline. It has even chosen to occupy this niche within the European construction. I doubt that this choice will be effective in the long term.

Faced with this entry into a comfortable financialisation, the productive sphere enlarged and deepened elsewhere, notably in the US and Germany. However, in the latter case this process produced different results. Arrighi analyses the evolution of Germany and stresses – in an extremely convincing way – facets of the German failure not hitherto perceived. While the rates of growth in industrial productivity were three times higher in Germany between 1870 and 1914 than those of Britain, in terms of per capita income the German acceleration was slow and modest. This difference starkly illustrates the thesis proposed by Arrighi and Braudel, that capitalism is not reducible to the market (or to the production behind the market); the benefits deriving from monopolies of power, including financial power, are great. However, they are also fragile, as we shall see below. The US, on the other hand, succeeded completely in supplanting

Great Britain. It did not, however, benefit from an advantage, financial or otherwise, associated with a dominant insertion into the global system until 1945. The US was constructed through an organisation of its industrial and agricultural productive spheres that was autocentred to a degree unknown in any other country at the time. Insulated in a continental territory, rich in resources of all kinds, and the beneficiary of the dominant global migratory flow, the US achieved more efficient forms of organisation of production. These were later to form the foundations of the country's global hegemony. Here again, Arrighi correctly highlights the fact that the large modern firm – the future multinational – started as, and often remains, a large integrated American firm. The analogy between this sort of construction and expansion and that of Russia is striking. The Russian empire, and then the Soviet Union, also constructed itself as a massive autocentred space at a certain remove from the world system. The failure was due not to this choice, analogous to that made by the US, but was simply, in my opinion, the result of internal factors – the backwardness of imperial Russia, the nature of Sovietism and its limits – and the century-long conflict (1880–1980) between Russia and Germany and then Russia and the US (with another between Russia and Germany still to come?).

The general financialisation of the global system which emerged from the 1880s onwards is a distinct phenomenon. The period 1873–96 was one of relative stagnation in the growth of production; this, associated with the permanent trend towards the concentration of capital, toppled the competitive form of the productive system, dominant until then, and ushered in a new oligopolistic form. Hobson, Hilferding and Lenin all emphasised in their different ways the importance of this qualitative change which leads me – with them – to see 1880 as a major turning point. The great depression of 1873–96 struck the old industrial centres (Great Britain, France and Belgium) while the growth of industrial production continued in new centres (Germany and the US), just as today recession has struck in the Triad (North America, Europe and, to a lesser and later extent, Japan) while industrialisation accelerates in east Asia (China, Korea and Southeast Asia). The old centres turned to the comfortable position of bankers of the world and financed a sort of delocalisation (especially in the direction of Russia, Austro-Hungary, the Ottoman empire and the white Commonwealth but less in the direction of their own colonies to which they would be forced to turn later). Analogous phenomena such as the debt trap of the Third World and eastern Europe can be seen in recent times. However, delocalisation, so prevalent in the 1970s that one could have believed that the world map of industrial implantation would be transformed (see Froebel, Heinrichs and Kreye 1980), proved to be of limited importance and duration. Since around 1980 recentralisation has operated to the benefit of the old centres of accumulation (but at a rhythm which has not led to the end of the long depression). It should also be noted that the parallel accelerated take-off in east Asia owes quantitatively little to foreign investment, although this plays an important role in the transfer of technology.

We understand, then, that late 19th-century financialisation took different forms in different countries. In Great Britain and France, the form was the cosmopolitan capitalist financier (like the Rothschilds), becoming more and more autonomous *vis-à-vis* the state, as Hobson remarked. It is true that this autonomy was only relative as one of the major sources of the surplus collected by this finance capital and placed on the exterior was that of colonial tribute. Bukharin and Lenin theorised this 'rentier' behaviour and proposed, on this basis, a critique of the new 'subjectivist' economic science. In Germany, on the other hand, financial capital coupled itself to industry, which continued its rapid take-off. Hilferding observed that this fusion of banking and industry allowed the country to be run as a single integrated enterprise, which one could term as monopolistic state capitalism or Germany Inc. (as Japan was later dubbed Japan Inc.). In contemporary capitalism this oligopolisation crystallised the conflicts which Lenin accurately termed as inter-imperialist (not to be reduced to conflicts over colonial empires), to which the two world wars bear witness. It was because Lenin thought that the proletariat would not put up with such conflict, and that consequently the world (or at least Europe) was on the verge of socialist revolution, that he termed this stage of imperialism the 'highest'. History proved him only partially right; revolution did occur in a semi-periphery, Russia ('the weak link'), but it did not spread to Europe. It extended itself rather to other peripheries in the east – both in a radical form (China) and an attenuated form (the national liberation movements of Asia and Africa) – and deployed itself in these ways from 1917 to 1975 (the end of the Bandung era, as I have already mentioned). However, imperialism had not entered its final stage. It survived and redeployed itself elsewhere in new forms.

The period of relative stagnation, the great depression of 1873–96 which preceded the First World War and continued into the interwar period, was thus a time of generalised financialisation. I mean by this that the period did not witness an incidence of geographically localised financialisation (as in the Italian towns or the United Provinces) but included all societies of the developed core. This phenomenon is analogous to that which has been occurring since 1980, which is here again associated with a stagnation in the expansion of productive systems. I will return to this new situation below but would repeat here what I said earlier regarding the contrast between the process M-M' and the process M-P-M'. The former is always a sign of crisis, that is to say at relative stagnation of P. It always produces results which are eventually insupportable, increasing inequalities in a manner that is so rapidly disastrous that the process is thrown into doubt by inevitable social and political struggles.

Is financialisation nevertheless a necessary stage in which the conditions for a new period of growth are re-established, as some theorists believe? This is a discourse which we currently hear repeated *ad nauseam*; structural adjustment must necessarily pass through a stage of financialisation. I do not share this point of view. I would say that on the contrary financialisation is a mode of crisis management, not the preparation for its end. This management, far from creating the conditions for a recovery, simply makes it more remote. Recovery sometimes occurs elsewhere but at a relative distance from the centre of financialisation. The financialisation of Europe from 1880 to 1945 did not help it to come out of recession. It was in the US, a little removed from this disastrous process, that the forces of renewed industrial progress were established. Are we today witnessing a contradictorily analogous process? Are the US, Japan and Europe, dragging Latin America and the Middle East behind them, becoming bogged down in both stagnation and financialisation while east Asia becomes the site of the next expansion of the productive system? I will discuss this hypothesis below.

Finally, to conclude this section, at the risk of repetition I would draw attention to the qualitative difference which separates the contradictory interrelationship of financialisation and the productive system in the mercantilist and industrial stages. In the mercantilist stage commerce is the driving force and its expansion creates the conditions necessary for an expansion of production. In the industrial stage the causality is reversed, a fact which the neoliberal high priests of the General Agreement on Tariffs and Trade (GATT) would never admit, and it is the expansion of production which permits the expansion of commerce. In the mercantilist stage the profits made from trade are reinvested wherever possible (that is to say wherever the expansion of production continues) in trade, and, when this is not possible, in financialisation (which is then accompanied by stagnation). In the following stage profits are reinvested in industry until this operation loses its *raison d'être* (its profitability) and then the financialisation reflex imposes itself, accompanied by stagnation. Thus rather than cycles of financialisation, I refer to specifically different phases of accumulation.

Globalisation since 1945

New forms

If I have noted the date 1945 (or 1950) as a turning point it is precisely because the forms of globalisation which prevailed in the post-war period are qualitatively different from those which predominated from 1880, in certain ways even from 1800.

I have discussed the particularities of the 1945–90 period sufficiently elsewhere not to need to repeat them (see Amin 1995). I will therefore simply recall that I have attributed the relatively strong growth that characterised all the regions of the world during this period to the three societal projects on which the postwar take-off was based: (1) the historic compromise of capital and labour, run in the framework of the national state developed by the practice of Keynesianism; (2) the Soviet project so-called socialist construction, autocentred and delinked from the world system (which I have analysed in terms of a project to construct a capitalism without capitalists); and (3) the modernist and developmentalist national bourgeois project of the Third World (which I have called the Bandung project for Asia and Africa, using the expression *desarrollismo* for Latin America), inscribing the industrialisation of these countries in a newly negotiated and revised global interdependence.

As well as the particularities clearly specific to each of these three pillars of the post-war world system, I have remarked on two characteristics which they have in common. The first is that each of these societal projects distances itself from extreme economic liberalism to associate the tasks and objectives of economic efficacy (in a global inter-dependence controlled to varying degrees) with that of an affirmation of a social framework allowing control of the market. This affirmation defined by the social hegemonies specific to each of these three groups of countries, proceeds from a rejection of the idea that markets are self regulating, and confirms the critique of free-market utopianism made by Karl Polanyi, after Marx and Keynes. The second is that the practice of policies and effective strategies in this framework is primarily conceived of as stemming from the national responsibility of the state and of national society, even though these strategies remain open to the exterior. The hegemony of the US, which I have described above, operated within the limits imposed by this framework, its strictly economic dimension – that is to say the technological advance of the US – was rapidly eroded by its own success through the expansion of the organisational form of the multinational in Europe and Japan. Therefore the three other aspects of this hegemony – control of the global monetary and financial system, military superiority and the cultural and linguistic deployment of the American way of life – have gradually assumed more importance. The first of these aspects of globalisation became exhausted by its own contradictions, thus leading, with the weakening of growth, to the stagnationist financialisation which was established after 1980 (which is thus another turning point). Effectively, the globalisation imposing itself on the national policies outlined above could first be seen in the fixed exchange rate system and the dollar standard. The progress of European construction and the Japanese take-off could not fail to cast doubt on this facet of

American hegemony even if, as I have written elsewhere (Amin 1995), no alternative to the dollar standard could be found and the crisis management (which has dominated policymaking since 1980) has delayed the response to this contradiction.

The second dimension – the militarisation of the system – is so clearly evident that it barely provokes comment. I have merely remarked that this military Keynesianism played an important part in the maintenance of rapid American and global growth. However, it could not become the most effective instrument of American hegemony until the phase itself had come to an end with the fall of the Soviet adversary. It remains true that this new supremacy is unparalleled in history: never before have weapons in general and one nation in particular been sufficiently powerful to envisage military intervention – albeit of an extremely destructive nature – on the level of the entire planet.

The third dimension of the new globalisation poses some relatively old questions in new terms. The tributary world system was shared between cultural areas which conserved their own characteristics; one can barely speak of universalism for those times, despite the universalist dimension of the great religions and philosophies which founded their cultures. Universalism appeared in 1500, with the Renaissance and then later the Enlightenment, although in the deformed and truncated form of the Eurocentrism which accompanied the biased fashioning of the new system by its European core. However, this universalism, which was to found the values of the modern world – positive ones such as democracy and negative ones such as economistic alienation – did not erase diversity within Europe. British hegemony, forced to accustom itself to the European balance of power, was thus not accompanied by an expansion of the English language. In the post-Second World War period, despite the marked nature of American hegemony, the strong national content of the strategies which defined the age maintained a degree of conciliation between universalism and political and cultural diversity. The contradiction specific to the cultural dimension of capitalist globalisation has thus only recently become apparent. It has often been attributed to the power of the media, which are responsible for the contraction of the world into a 'global village'. This reality must certainly not be left out of the picture of globalisation.

However, it merely highlights what had been the case for a long time: ancient cultures (tributary, including those of the European Middle Ages) have long since disappeared and been absorbed by capitalist culture, defined here by its essential content – economistic alienation – and not by its European origin and form. However, this universal capitalist culture has never been able to impose a universal legitimacy, because it accompanies and sustains a polarised world system. The accentuation and affirmation of capitalist culture through the modern media, together with the aggravation of polarisation after the post-war societal projects had exhausted their potential, have brought the cultural question to the fore and led to desperate quests to rediscover cultural identity in the Third World. The dominant linguistic form of this expression of capitalist cultural domination, produced by American hegemony, meets resistance even in Europe, particularly in France.

In the analysis of the post-war system that I propose – whether it be in its ascendant phase or the current crisis – neither the structure of the system as a whole, nor that of its constituent parts, nor a potential hegemony is wholly or even principally determined by the 'competition of firms in the market', as the dominant ideology of economic reductionism would have us believe. These structures in themselves do not concern the intermediate level in the Braudelian sense; with Marx, Polanyi, Braudel and others, I consider them to be the product of the interrelated functioning of the intermediate and higher levels. Competition leads to opposition between states as much as between enterprises because capitalism is inseparable from the modern state; they have become inseparable through simultaneous development, and they control together the structures of accumulation. In this spirit, as Arrighi has written, if territorialism means enlarging the sphere dominated by a particular capitalism (a component of the world system), modes of action simultaneously exist which allow the intensification of accumulation in a restricted zone (these modes of action are the control of trade, technological innovation military superiority, cultural influence and financialisation). The variable combination of these two modes of accumulation explains how small states (the Italian towns, the Netherlands) come to occupy important places in the system (but are never, in my sense of the term, hegemonic), how large states frequently do not achieve this pre-eminence and indeed are often swamped by the system, and how hegemony remains the exception among those states which effectively articulate the two modes. As Vergopoulos wrote (1993), what appears to be competition between firms is in fact competition between national systems from which firms gain their momentum (these systems establish the productive capacities of the labour force and many other things without which commercial competitiveness could not exist).

Economics is inseparable from politics. The events of every day confirm this in a way that is more than obvious. It is difficult to imagine Japan becoming hegemonic, for instance, because, despite the efficiency of its firms, it is militarily vulnerable and lacks cultural influence. Thus since 1985 we have seen the financial surplus of Japan loaned to the US with the debt serviced in devalued dollars, the operation settled by an enormous drain on Japan's surplus made by its competitor (Arrighi 1994). Thus we see the external budget deficit of the US absorbing surplus on a global scale, absorbing the means which the nations of the Third World try to attract in vain for use in their own development. We have even seen the rich oil producers of the Gulf finance their own military conquest by Washington. There is little hope that the financial placements of these countries in external markets can ever be recovered. Conversely, during the two world wars, the US reversed its financial position – from debtor to creditor – by effectively appropriating the property of its competitors.

The world is thus structured as much by interstate relations as by the play of private commercial competition. It even tends, perhaps, to be so to a greater degree. For instance, while previous monetary systems (the sterling standard for example) were largely run by private high finance, Bretton Woods placed the 'production of money' under the control of a network of governmental agencies, including those of international status (the International Monetary Fund, IMF), themselves led by the Federal Reserve System. It is true that this tendency towards increasing state domination could be reversed, as indeed it was between the years 1968 and 1973. Since then Eurodollars have renewed the autonomy of financial flows as the prelude to the great reprivatisation on the basis of which the current financialisation took off (after 1980). However, it must be noted that this change corresponded with

US political decline following its defeat in Vietnam; this encouraged the Third World to go on the offensive, the most illustrious example being that of the Organisation of Petroleum-Exporting Countries (OPEC). It must also be noted that the success of the American counter-offensive aimed at restoring its hegemony is based to a large extent on its military supremacy (in the light of the success of the Gulf War and the collapse of the Soviet Union, the Europeans, for instance, show that they can achieve nothing without the US, either in Yugoslavia, or the ex-USSR, or even in Somalia). It is thanks to this military superiority that the US has been able to impose the dollar standard despite the decline in its commercial efficacy.

The firm–state relationship is not, however, linear; it functions in both directions, in some phases to the benefit of one, in others to the benefit of the other. For instance, in Lenin's age the 'monopolies' were certainly the instruments of state expansion, as were American multinationals after the Second World War. In the current phase, however, these firms have freed themselves from the powers of states and limited the effectiveness of state interventions. Is this a structural characteristic of the new globalisation and is it liable to become stabilised as such? Or is it a characteristic contingent on crisis?

The institutionalisation of the organisation of the world system is not altogether new. Here I share the general point of view of the world-system school which sees it as an essential characteristic of historical capitalism (what I call actually existing capitalism, as opposed to the imaginary ideal of ideological capitalism). From the Treaty of Westphalia (1648), which fixed the initial rules which were renewed at the Congress of Vienna (1815) and then by the Treaty of Versailles (1919) – which took a further step with the founding of the League of Nations – to the creation of the United Nations in 1945, this institutionalisation is in constant progress. Whenever it appears paralysed by the incoherence of policies, as has been the case since 1980 due to worsening crisis, we immediately witness attempts, by gatherings such as the G7, to overcome this incoherence. The dysfunctionalising nature of the contradictions is such, however, as I proposed in my analysis of the management of the crisis (Amin, 1995: Part 1), that instruments appear wholly incapable of meeting the challenge.

The post-war period is clearly not homogeneous in terms of patterns of growth, made up as it is of a long phase of growth (1945–68) followed by a long crisis (1971–). The sub-phase of transition from 1968 (major political events) to 1971 (suppression of the gold convertibility of the dollar) can be clearly demarcated. Financialisation took off later in conjunction with the political transformation inaugurated by Reagan and Thatcher. The years 1985–90 (the collapse of Sovietism) mark another cut-off point, just as the years 1975 (the 'new world order' project proposed by the Third World) to 1982 (the Third World's first financial crisis which broke in Mexico) marked the end of the Bandung project and the renewed expansion of the comprador class in the peripheries. It remains difficult, in my opinion, to determine the precise significance of these dates: the events are too recent for us to judge their true importance. Do they define the end of a long phase (1800–1950 or 1800–1990) or merely the transition from one sub-phase to another? the judgement that we make regarding future possibilities depends on the answers that we give to these questions through analysis of the crisis and its management.

Globalisation and the continuing accumulation crisis

The controlled globalisation of the period 1945–90 has come to an end due to the exhaustion of the phase of accumulation which sustained it.

I have tried to analyse elsewhere (Amin et al., 1993), in some detail, the processes by which the erosion and then the collapse of the three pillars supporting the completed phase of accumulation led to the current crisis. In this endeavour I believed it useful to highlight the new characteristics of the productive system – which is in the process of becoming globalised (as opposed to internationalised) – and the new contradiction arising from this fact: the space of production is becoming globalised while the spheres of political and social management remain limited by the political frontiers of states.

I do not mean to imply here that unbridled economic globalisation – which pushed neoliberal ideology to its extreme – could impose itself on and overcome the resistance of politics, which would be forced to submit or, in the current terminology, adjust.

107

On the contrary I have developed the thesis that this new form of economistic capitalist utopia is doomed to failure.

As it does not create the conditions for a new system of accumulation, the unbridled globalisation that the existing powers are trying to impose effectively reduces economic policies to the status of crisis management policies. I have proposed interpreting the ensemble of measures employed – liberalisation without frontiers, financial globalisation, floating exchange rates, high interest rates, the external budget deficit of the US, the external debt of the southern and eastern countries – as a perfectly coherent set of crisis management policies offering financial placements to capital which would otherwise be massively devalued through the lack of any profitable outlet in the expansion of systems of production. The process of financialisation is thus overwhelming, with the expanding process M-M' substituting itself for the defunct process M-P-M'.

Contemporary financialisation is thus once again merely the sign of a crisis of accumulation rather than its solution.

However, by dint of its completely generalised nature, embracing each and every segment of the world system, financialisation has acquired an unprecedented dimension. What future is taking shape behind the smoke screen that it puts up? What new system of accumulation is putting itself, or not putting itself, into place? We are here in a field where all – or nearly all – hypotheses are possible, where all scenarios are imaginable; such is the uncertainty of the future and so fragile are our fragments of knowledge concerning the recomposition of the world. The future of globalisation remains a great unknown.

Three approaches can be employed to explore this uncertain future. The first, which is very much *à la mode*, is based on chaos theory. Progress in the mathematics of non-linear functions has led to the discovery that minimal differences in the parameters of some of these functions produce gigantic differences in their subsequent development. This discovery certainly clashes with the spontaneous intuition that small differences at the start cannot engender great differences in what follows. Chaos functions explain natural phenomena which cannot otherwise be accounted for. Could the discovery also be relevant to the social sciences? Undoubtedly, functions of this type could contribute to the analysis of a number of economic and social phenomena, through analogy with other natural phenomena. The currency markets, for instance, can be conceived of as presenting chaotic structures of an analogous or similar nature. However, I am still of the philosophical opinion that changes to the whole of society cannot be studied with the help of conceptual tools of this type. The philosophy of history, historical materialism among other approaches, is still irreplaceable.

The second approach is that of the historians of capitalism, notably in the world system current, who emphasise either recurrences or the flexibility of the system or both. I have several reservations regarding this approach, preferring to highlight what is qualitatively new after each turning point, thus relegating recurrences as merely apparent and rejecting the idea of cycles. The fact is that the future can never be correctly predicted at the decisive turning points, which only emerge as such with hindsight. Would a Venetian merchant of 1350 have been able to answer the question, 'Are you creating capitalism?' It thus seems to me that if 1990 (or 1980) constitutes a new turning point – and that it does is merely my intuition – it is extremely difficult to know how the world will recompose itself after. We must, however, try to make a judgement because action to safeguard the future of the human race depends on it. Getting it wrong is a risk that must be taken.

I will use a method which remains wholly relevant, that of historical materialism. I would draw the conclusion from the examination of the phase 1945–90 that the old form of polarisation (the contrast between the industrialised cores and non-industrialised peripheries, dominant from 1800 to 1950) has been progressively left behind by the industrialisation, however unequal this may have been, of the eastern and southern peripheries. In these conditions the globalised law of value defined for the period 1800–1950 must be revised to account for this qualitative transformation. I have done this by proposing a new framework for its operation (Amin 1994c), defined by what I have referred to as the five monopolies on which the new forms of polarisation are based (these monopolies are control over finance, technology, the earth's resources, the media and weapons of mass destruction). I refer the reader back to these definitions.

That having been said, it is not the case that the new structure of a polarised system based on the efficient use of these five monopolies can be effectively constructed. All the problems of the future associated with the recomposition (or decomposition) of the ex-USSR, with the take-off of east Asia (most importantly China), with the stagnation of the west and its American and African appendages and with the recomposition (or failure) of the European Union can be found here.

It is not my intention to return here to the set of evolutions which led the post-war system into crisis, or to the diverse interpretations of these events. I would rather refer the reader here to some of the major works on the subject, notably to François Chesnais (1994), Giovanni Arrighi (1994), Michel Beaud (1989) and the article of Kostas Vergopoulos (1993). I share the points of view developed in these works so fully that a repetition of their arguments would not be useful here. I would add only my own works on the subject, *Empire of Chaos* (1992b) and *La Gestion capitaliste de la crise* (1995). The opposing argument – the defence of financialisation – is developed *ad nauseam* in the dominant literature. The only work to which I wish to refer here is the excellent book by Olivier Pastré (1992), whose fine argument poses certain questions which cannot be ignored. I would add to this some of Michel Aglietta's book (1986).

It is thus simply necessary to recall briefly what appears to me to be solidly established regarding the important new characteristics of the post-war system. I would note here the following.

First, the undeniable deepening of interdependence – over and above commercial exchanges – not only in the organisation of processes of production, but more in its extension to fields previously less affected, such as service industries. However, if the tendency is clearly towards dismantling the coherence of the national systems of production on which historical capitalism was founded, there has been little progress, as Vergopoulos notes (1993), towards the substituting of a coherent globalised productive system. It must also be remembered that globalisation as it is today remains fragile and vulnerable, and that if its evolution is not mastered by the establishment of a progressive social framework which is capable of operating effectively and coherently at all levels, from the national to the global, then regressions of all sorts are not only possible but probable. Far from leading to a sort of integrated super-imperialism à la Kautsky, globalisation accentuates potential conflicts, deconstructing and reconstructing the ground on which states and firms confront each other. Will capitalism be capable of meeting the challenge?

Second, the emergence of new organisational forms of the firm and its relationship with its economic environment: sub-contracting in its numerous forms and leasing have enriched the spectrum of strategies available to firms to an unprecedented extent. Later in the post-war period, with the onset of crisis and financialisation, this transformation of the potential strategic options of firms has reduced the hitherto well-established distinction between financial and industrial actors. Firms develop mixed strategies, productive and financial. This is one of the major elements of what I have termed as generalised financialisation.

Third, the strong tendencies set in motion by the qualitative evolutions noted here operate as forces of exclusion, running from exclusion within even the richest societies to the exclusion on the global level of entire continents, such as Africa.

Faced with these new challenges, the dominant powers have only given responses which exacerbate the consequences. With the erosion of the three post-war models training the market (local and global), which I have analysed elsewhere in terms of the exhaustion of anti-Fascist ideology (Amin 1995), the conditions have been recreated in which dominant capital tries to impose unilaterally the utopian logic of managing the world as a market, through the ensemble of the currently prevalent deregulation policies. As has been said, globalisation serves to dismantle the national social contracts produced through centuries of social struggle without providing any significant replacement on either a global or regional scale (on the scale of the European Union for instance).

As I (Amin 1995) and others (for example, Chesnais 1994) have frequently written, this response which is not a response has led to global financialisation. The depression is expressed by the enormous growth in surpluses of capital which cannot find any profitable outlet in the expansion of the productive system. The major, perhaps even exclusive, preoccupation of the dominant powers is to find financial outlets for these surpluses in order to avoid the catastrophe (for the system) of their, massive devaluation. I have suggested that the coherence of the national and worldwide policies currently being pursued stems from this factor – privatisation, deregulation, high interest rates, floating exchange rates, the American policy of systematic external deficit, the debt burden of the Third World, etc. I will not return to this point here. In its turn this global financialisation becomes locked into a regressionary cycle. By its own momentum the system gives to financier-rentier capital the opportunity of always ensuring that its own interests prevail over the general interest, whatever the cost might be for national and global economics. The incredible growth of inequalities of income, at all levels from the local to the global, produced by the increasing hold of income from sources other than production (that is, financial rent) over relatively stagnant production fully expresses the irrationality of the system. Are the counter-measures proposed by way of damage limitation at all effective? The outcome of these counter-measures appears to be regionalisation, the virtues of which are currently being trumpeted by the media, whether it be the inexorable construction of Europe or other initiatives (the North American Free Trade Area (NAFTA), the Asia–Pacific project, etc). I have proposed a critical interpretation of these projects, to which I refer the reader (Amin, 1995). The European project appears to me to have entered a period of turbulence which could still throw its future into doubt, not only following the internal imbalance created by the unification of Germany but more and especially because, conceived by the Right, the European Union remains a project of market integration without a social dimension that can establish at EU level the equivalent of the historic compromise of labour and capital at the national levels. I have proposed similarly critical interpretations of the market integration projects of other regions of the world (see Amin 1995: Part 3).

Conclusion: an extremely uncertain future

To explore the alternatives concerning this uncertain future, as a conclusion to this debate on globalisation, it seems necessary to return to the central question of method defined at the beginning of our discussion: the question of the law of value and of the relationship between the economic law of the capitalist system and the functioning of its politics.

The law of value considered at its most abstract level, or at the level of abstraction defining its globalised form, operates at the intermediate level in Braudel's terminology (that is, in the framework of the market). In Marx's conceptualisation, the law of value defines the dominance of the economic sphere over the social, political and cultural spheres, without separating the one from the others. The law of value dictates not only the economic life of the capitalist world but, as I have said, all aspects of its social life as well. It thus plunges its roots into Braudel's elementary level, which indeed it fashions, but also projects itself onto the higher level of power. However, domination of one level of authority does not imply suppression of the others; otherwise the world would effectively be reducible to the 'market' (or to firms and the market), as the dominant ideology proposes. The system of prices, which determines the distribution of wealth, is necessarily different from the system of values. This stems not only from market imperfections but essentially from the influence of power over the market, the higher level over the intermediate level, political authority over economic authority. Because this dialectic does not interest them, all moderate empiricists ignore value, not wishing to see in it anything but a smokescreen which hides the only reality which they wish to know, the immediate. Arrighi's excellent book, *The Long Twentieth Century*, gives us startling examples of the disparities between the production of value and the distribution of wealth in history. He looks beneath the surface of the system and shows us why and how industrialist Germany did not achieve the opulence of financialised England, how earlier the Italian towns and the Netherlands captured the world's riches, and how later the US met the offensives of Japan, etc. In a study on the globalisation of the footwear industry, Gereffi and Korzeniewicz (1990) show that the profit which returns to the delocalised producers is tiny compared with that gathered by the big brand names which dominate commercial circles: a fine example of the disparity between apportionment of value, created by producers, and that of wealth, dictated by prices, profits and rents. I have myself, in my analysis of the 'future of polarisation' (Amin 1994c), expressed the idea that due to the five monopolies of the core (technology, finance, access to resources, culture, armaments), the very success of industrialisation in the peripheries would go along with increased polarisation of wealth. The five monopolies of the core are clearly manifestations of political, social, cultural and ideological power rather than the results of market mechanisms.

I envisage exploring the possibilities concerning the future, then, by putting into practice what I consider to be the essential elements of the historical materialist project. There are two possible scenarios, of an extreme nature, or more precisely two families of scenarios each presenting a range of diverse modalities. The possibility of cross-breeding also exists and is perhaps the most probable in real life. The worst-case scenario is that which prolongs the dominant system as it is, or merely adopts variants which are only partially corrective. The major characteristic here is that firms (capital) would free themselves from powers, and indeed come to use, or at least neutralise, power themselves. Arrighi notes here that today's multinationals escape from the laws of states just as commercial dealings in medieval fairs ecaped from local feudal laws. Personally I do not believe that such an order can be long-lasting as it generates nothing but chaos and its effects are so disastrous that it will inevitably engender reactions strong enough to destroy it. In a polemical tone, I will thus take up the words of Arrighi: if this order must marginalise entire continents and reduce the majority of humanity to poverty, then which are redundant – people or the laws of capital?

The modalities of such a schema of lasting chaos can be easily imagined: an isolationist Triad (North America, Europe and Japan) and generalised apartheid, punctuated by occasional genocides in order to secure the position of the possessors and protect their fortresses. However, even in this extreme case, would not the Triad be forced in its turn practically to tear itself apart? A permanent hegemony – and that of the US is the only one conceivable – would be necessary to avoid intra-Triad conflict or even the renewal of intra-European conflict. The rule of every man for himself does not create compromise and harmony but rather their opposite. The schema outlined here corresponds nicely with US president Ronald Reagan's vision. In record time he seems to have already returned from the past; it was, as Arrighi writes, a very short 'belle epoque'.

One possible scenario in this framework would be the installation of the West in illusory short-term comfort while oriental Asia continued to progress at a removal from this preposterous form of globalisation-exclusion. This oriental Asia would perhaps include Japan ('returning to its roots') which, cushioned by its technological advance, would reconnect itself to China and the other industrialised countries of the region. Or of course Japan could remain in the sphere of the western Triad as China pursues growth without trying to become integrated into the Japanese sphere. The US desire to integrate one and all, that is Japan, China, Korea, etc, in its own renovated sphere now called Asia-Pacific, amounts to no more than wishful thinking in my opinion. In fact the Asia-Pacific sphere could become no more than a supplementary force separating Japan and China. Whatever the specific scenario, where is this new industrialisation of Asia (east Asia, Southeast Asia and India) leading us? If Asia remains in the global system, we again find here the law of value, the five monopolies and the new polarisation. Or, of course, Asia could delink itself in the sense in which I use the term. This is not impossible.

In all these modalities there are nevertheless too many dangers for the solidity of the structures that carry them to be credible. The Africans, Arabs, Muslims and Latin Americans will surely, one day or another, find effective means to serve notice of their existence. The Europeans and North Americans, who have not proved in history to be completely inert, or to be devoid of a sense of initiative and generosity, would not accept for long the role that the schema of a new Middle Ages would reserve for them, and especially not the role reserved for their own working classes – progressive exclusion from comfort. However, if the left is not on the scene to mobilise them around a credible and possible incremental programme, then their revolt could see them lurch to the Right and neo-Fascism. This also, of course, has a historical precedent.

One cannot thus avoid the political question concerning the incremental strategies that must be developed to meet the challenge. Globalisation implies that if a problem is global then its solution must also be so. It is one thing to recognise this fact but quite another to advocate passive submission to the requirements of globalisation in the form that imposes itself while waiting for … Godot? Global revolution? The miraculous progress that this could bring for a while? My thesis is simple: globalisation advances progressively, but according to the diverse modalities imposed upon it by political and social struggles. It can thus be set on a track leading to the solution of the problems that it poses or on a track leading to sclerosis and disaster. The task of political strategy is to seize hold of the margins of possible action, however slender they might be, in order to extend the autonomy of future choices.

In this perspective, could one define the stage immediately to come while accepting certain aspects of the extant liberalism, indeed even of financialisation? Arrighi and Pastré both appear to imagine so, in different terms. Arrighi insists on the recurring character of moments of 'liberalisation' (meaning the weakening of state efficacy), globalisation and even financialisation which, even if associated in a way with a crisis of the system (with a phase of accumulation which has run out of steam), is also, on the other hand, a necessary transition to another phase of accumulation. Pastré emphasises the possible progressive recompositions which could not only accommodate themselves to the new structures which are taking shape behind financialisation but even mobilise them for a new social contract. I take this apparently liberal but just as much social (in the sense of being socially progressive) argument absolutely seriously. Pastré imagines a social contract for France encompassing a decisive financial intervention in the institutional investors, which comprise the national savings, social savings, pensions, etc. This renewed social dialectic would ensure competition, due in part to a growing emphasis on education and research.

I do not object in any way in principle to this incremental project, which I would refer to as 'new social democracy' (which, like any social democracy, can be conceived of as an end in itself or as a staging post on the way to the more distant socialist objective). However, I believe it is useful to specify the conditions of its success, which are far from being met. Even at the level of France – as this country is the subject of the reflection in question – the project implies political and ideological trends which are not those taking shape in the current chaos. Furthermore, if we accept France's insertion into Europe, the project implies analogous trends in all France's principal EU partners. The new social democracy must be European or it cannot exist. It is what I would call giving the EU the social dimension which it lacks and which the strategy produced spontaneously by dominant capital does not yield. This contradiction is, in my opinion, absolutely capable of making Europe implode and eventually smashing all the hopes invested in it. Furthermore, the project sketched out by Pastré, accepting globalisation in principle, implies an organisation of the relationships between Europe and the other partners of the world system (the US, Japan and the gigantic peripheries of the three continents) which would support the deployment of its socially progressive logic rather than clashing its hopes. I would call this the construction of a polycentric world, which calls for a reorganisation of global markets such as to change the direction of the expansion of productive systems. This reorganisation thus enters into conflict with the principles of unbridled financialisation. In my opinion, this financialisation – linked to the crisis of accumulation and to a large extent produced by it – does not pave the way for an end to the crisis but merely deepens its contradictions. In the same way this reorganisation implies the negotiation of market shares open to the newly industrialising peripheral regions. It thus contradicts the principles which, in the name of liberalism, protect the monopolies in place in all their hostility to change. Finally, it implies a reorganisation of monetary systems, itself implying conflict with the principles on which the current financialisation rests (floating exchange rates, financial liberalisation on a global scale, etc).

Because of the gigantic difficulties with which these reorganisations are confronted in the real world I believe that the aspect of financialisation as a mode of crisis management will prevail over the potential dimensions which could allow it to become a moment of transition to a more socially progressive mode of accumulation on both the local and global levels.

What, then, are we left with? The prospect of another social system, abandoning the sacrosanct institution of private property, and of another globalisation, rejecting polarisation, remains the only alternative. The completion of such a project is certainly not conceivable in the short term and could look so distant as to seem utopian. I am not of this opinion. I even believe that the guiding principles of the policies which would constitute the first step of this long march can already be sketched out. I see this first step as the construction of a polycentric world allowing the reconstruction of progressive social contracts encompassing the management of the market. We are referring to a vision of the transition to global socialism which is very different from the perspective of the successive Internationals. I refer the reader back to these. History is not fashioned by the law of accumulation alone. Its path is fashioned by the conflict between this law and the logic of its negation.

This chapter is an edited version of a paper that was first published in 1996 as 'The challenge of globalisation', Review of International Political Economy, *vol. 3, no. 2, pp. 216–59.*

References

Aglietta, M. (1986) *La fin des devises*, Paris, La Decouverte

Amin, S. (1988) *Eurocentrism*, London, Zed Books

——(1991) 'The ancient world system versus the modern capitalist world system', *Review* xiv: 349–86

——(1992a) 'Capitalism et système-monde', *Sociologie et Societes* vol. 14, no. 2, pp. 181–202

——(1992b) *Empire of Chaos*, New York, MR Press

——(1994a) *Re-reading the Postwar Period: An Intellectual Itinerary*, New York, MR Press

——(1994b) *L'Ethnic à l'assaut des nations*, Paris, L'Harmattan

——(1994c) 'The future of global polarisation', *Review*, vol. 17, no. 3, pp. 337–47

——(1995) *La Gestion capitaliste de la crise*, Paris, L'Harmattan

Amin, S., Casanova, P.G. et al. (1993) *Mondialisation et accumulation*, Paris, L'Harmattan

Arrighi, G. (1994) *Mythes et paradoxes de l'histoire economique*, Paris, La Decouverte

Bairoch, Paul (1994) *Révolution industrielle et sous développement*, Paris, Mouton

Beaud, M. (1989) *L'Economie mondiale dans les annees 1980*, Paris, La Decouverte

Braudel, F. (1979) Civilisation and Capitalism, 15–18th Centuries, 3 vols, New York, Harper & Row

Chesnais, François (1994) *The Globalisation of Capital*, Paris, Syros Editions

Froebel, F. Heinrichs, J., and Kreye, O. (1980) *The New International Labour*, Cambridge, Cambridge University Press

Gereffi, G. and Korzeniewicz, M. (1990) 'Commodity, chains and the footwear exports in the semi-periphery', in Martin' W. G. (ed),

Semiperiphery States in the World Economy, New York, Greenwood Press

Marseille, J. (1984) *Empire colonial et capitalisme français*, Paris, Albin Michel

Pastré, O. (1992) *Les Nouveaux Piliers de la finance*, Paris, La Decouverte

Polanyi, K. (1994[1994]) *The Great Transformation: The Political and Economic Origins of Our Time*, Boston, MA, Beacon Hill

Vergopoulos, K. (1993) *Le nouveau système mondial*, Paris, Futur Anterlem

Wallerstein, I. (1974) *The Modern World System: Capitalist Agriculture and the Origins of the World Economy in the Sixteenth Century*, New York, NY, Academic Press

 4

History conceived as an eternal cycle

The theses of André Gunder Frank

In his 1998 work (*ReORIENT: Global Economy in the Asian Age*) André Gunder Frank returns to, and expands on, the thesis which he treated in his previous work written in 1993 in collaboration with Barry Gills, *The World System: Five Hundred Years or Five Thousand?*, with an emphasis on modern times (1500 to date). The thesis itself summarises the following fundamental proposals:

1. History is, from its inception, dealing with a system that has always been global, in the sense that the evolution of the various regions has never been determined by the interaction of forces internal to the societies in question but by forces operating on the global system, and that consequently, all efforts to write the history of a region of the world (Europe, China, or any other region) can only be illusory, since there is only one history, that of the one and only world system.

2. This world system has fundamentally remained the same ever since, and that consequently, successive modes or phases (such as those initiated in 1500 and 1800) do not exist and that the attempt to mark out qualitatively different phases based, for example, on the recognition of successive modes of production, is, as a result, misleading.

3. This world history evolves in a cyclical manner.

On the basis of these fundamental principles, Frank transposes a whole set of issues on the relative position of Europe and Asia in the modern age. Frank asserts here that:

1. The position of Asia (China, India, the Middle East) had been dominant until around 1800 and that it was only after this date that Europe (and the United States) began to assert their economic, political and military superiority.
2. The rise of the West cannot be explained by the construction of a new world system bound for conquest of the globe (as declared by the theses on the world economy, according to Frank) but by the involvement of Europe in the world system as it was (centred on Asia), the West, through this involvement, benefiting from the prevailing Asian crisis to usurp the latter's place during the two centuries that followed (from 1800 to today).
3. We are presently witnessing a repeat of the same scenario now operating in reverse to the advantage of Asia which, through its involvement in the world system, takes advantage of the crisis in the West and, without doubt, will regain the dominant position that had been hers in the world system before 1800, and by so doing complete the cycle.

Frank equally declares that any attempt at a theoretical construction which ignored the three fundamental principles cited earlier is inevitably Eurocentric, irrespective of whether it is the ideas of Marx (and the more modest ideas of Samir Amin), of the world economy (Wallerstein et al.), or of Weber, Sombart, Polanyi, Said, Bernal, and the whole lot.

Frank's assertion on these fundamental theses mentioned earlier is summarised by their author in a forceful manner.

> [W]e need a global perspective to ... perceive, – 'The Rise of the West', 'the development of capitalism', 'the hegemony of Europe', 'the rise and fall of great powers' ... 'the East Asian miracle' .... None of these were caused only or even primarily through the structure or interaction of forces 'internal' to any of the above. All of them were part and parcel of the structure and development of a single world economic system. (Frank 1998, p. 4)

And, to clarify that it is the same identical old world system, he writes:

> [T]he 'modern capitalist world-system' was not the reinvention but the continuation of Abu-Lughod's version of the same world system already in existence since at least 1250 ... [T]hen why not earlier? (1998, p. xix)

Just as he adds that the 'focus on "modes of production" only diverts our attention from the much more importantly defining world system ...' (1998, p. 24).

One is therefore, certainly dealing with an identical twin system for the most part, which has never undergone any qualitative transformation: 'There was no unilinear "progression" from one "mode" of production to another; but all manner of relations of production were and remain widely intermingled even within any one "society," not to mention the world society as a whole' (1998, p. 331). Frank further asserts that debates on the nature of systems (feudal, capitalist) are using 'procrustean and empty categories' (1998, p. 336) because the reality is that 'historical continuity has been far more important than any and all discontinuities' (1998, p. 342). Presented in this way, this continuity does not rhyme with the cyclical form it embraces, and which Frank justifies in general philosophical terms: 'Cyclical motion seems to be a universal fact of existence, life and being...' (1998, p. 347).

These theses are, in my opinion, not only false, but impotent. By adopting them, one prohibits oneself in advance from analysing the specificity of modes of organisation of society, and one renounces asking a series of questions on the workings of the various aspects of society (the economic life, the social power system and politics, etc). This gives rise to a split image of history, where nothing else exists except facts juxtaposed one on the other. Frank's work is a beautiful example, alas, of this kind of flattened history. The 'world system' which he describes is in fact reduced to a network of interregional trading links. The composition and the volume of these exchanges are therefore determined by the 'relative competitiveness' of producers, which are directly influenced by the combination of natural resources, more or less, of human labour and technology. It is the vision of the economic life that the standard view of economics offers us generally. The work is completely silent on everything that concerns the political organisation of the societies in question, or the current idea systems which legitimise power and the issues at stake. On the contrary, of course, I assert the decisive importance of the affirmation that the capitalist mode of production represents a qualitative rupture with systems that preceded it (including Europe of course). We are then obliged to specify: (1) the exact definition of the specificity of capitalism; (2) the date from which capitalism can be considered to be constituted; (3) the stages and shapes of its evolution.

In his work, Frank asks us to reappraise three centuries of mercantilism (1500–1800) founded on his central thesis, seeking to convince us that there has always been only one economy – the world economy – and that the latter has always been driven by the same logic over space and time. Based on this assumption, Frank takes up the issue of the 'rise of the West'. The sequence of his reasoning is as follows: (1) Europe created nothing new during these three centuries, only imitating what had already existed in Asia; (2) and in doing so, Europe continued to lag behind its model until the 19th century; (3) Europe featured in this world economy very marginally, and only began to integrate into it seriously during the period under consideration; (4) Europe was able to do so through the precious metals extracted from America to close its trade deficit with the more advanced Asia. Frank develops what he hopes is a striking comparison between this model of the 'rise of Europe on the back of Asia' by way of its integration into the erstwhile world system (during the Asiacentric era) and that of contemporary Asia that operates in the same way by its growing involvement in the contemporary world system (henceforth centred on the West–Europe beefed up by the United States).

Citing Wallerstein (1997, p. 252), 'Entrepreneurs or companies who make large profits ... by being simultaneously producers, merchants and financiers ...', Frank adds: 'Of course, but Wallerstein fails to observe that the same was and is equally true throughout the world economy and not only in the small European "capitalist" part' (1998, p. 31). Furthermore, in this imitation, Europe continues to lag behind in relation to its Asiatic models. Frank writes: 'Europe was certainly not central to the world economy before 1800.... [The] Chinese Ming/Qing, Indian

Mughal, and even Persian Safavid and Turkish Ottoman empires carried much greater political and even military weight than any or all of Europe' (1998, p. 5). And again:

> The world economy continued to be dominated by Asians for at least three centuries more, until about 1800. Europe's relative and absolute marginality in the world economy continued, despite Europe's new relations with the Americas, which it used to increase its relations with Asia.... Productive and commercial economic activities, and population growth ... also continued to expand faster and more in Asia until at least 1750 ... (1998, p. 53)

'Europe was not a major industrial centre in terms of exports to the rest of the world economy' (1998, p. 177). The weak and inferior position of Europe, which is certainly rooted in its delayed scientific and technological take-off, makes its 'industries' non-competitive (I will come back to this inappropriate qualification that Frank uses). Frank goes on: 'All serious inquiries .... show that this "stage" (superiority of Europe's science and technology) did not begin until the second half of the 19th century ... that is two centuries after the scientific "revolution" and one after the industrial "revolution"' (1998, p. 190). Frank completes this affirmation by expatiating on developments concerning the use of sophisticated financial mechanisms in the management of trade and credit practised in Asia (1998, p. 210 onwards). Generalising the assertion, he says: '[The] Asians were no more "traditional" than Europeans and in fact largely far less so' (1998, p. 259). Also, it is not surprising that the volume and density of merchandise trade remained much stronger in Asia than in the rest of the world. Thus, in 1750 and 1800, Asian production was much greater, and it was more productive and competitive than anything the Europeans and the Americas were able to muster ...' (1998, p. 172).

Frank notes, for example, that Chinese internal trade in grains was ten to fifteen times greater than the 'normal' trade of the Baltic (1998, p. 222). Frank asserts, forcefully, the centrality of Asia in the world system of the time. '[I]f anything, the modern world system was under Asian hegemony, not European' (1998, p. 166).

Nonetheless, Eurocentric prejudice points to the contrary: 'Yet the mythology has grown up that world trade was created by and dominated by the Europeans, even in Asia' (1998, p. 178). Therefore, mercantile Europe invented nothing, not anything better than what contemporary Asia invented anew when it integrated further in the contemporary system. Europe was content to integrate into the system of the Asiacentric era. The means used to achieve this end was gold and money from the Americas. Frank summarises his thesis thus: '[T]he Europeans bought themselves a seat ... on the Asian train...' (1998, p. 277).

Displaying a map indicating the movement of international transactions of the time (1998, p. 65), backed up by numerous references on their volume, noting the European trade deficit (gold and money representing two-thirds of these exports – the chart on 1998, p. 148), Frank summarises his thesis with a beautiful sentence: Europe built itself by 'climbing up on Asian shoulders' (1998, p. 277). Furthermore, money transferred from America to Asia via the European trade deficit was in no way 'buried' in Asia as Eurocentric prejudice would have it. It was used to strengthen the expansion of Asian production and trade. The money going into Asia 'did oil the wheels of production and trade and was not just "dug up in the Americas to be buried again in Asia"' (1998, p. 138).

In reference to this issue, he cites Wallerstein who said: '[B]ullion brought into Asia was largely used for hoarding and jewellery ... [This is] evidence that the East Indies remained external to the European world-economy...' (Frank, 1998, p. 153). Frank takes up the other side of this argument: 'For, contrary to Wallerstein, the world-wide flow of money to Asia ... is evidence that they were parts of the same world economy ...' (1998, p. 153). In Asia the increased arrival of money 'did not substantially raise prices as it did in Europe ... [Instead] it generated increased production and transactions ...' (1998, p. 157). In China, 'merchants advanced capital (presumably ... derived from exports and the import of silver) to peasant producers in return for later receipt of their crops' (1998, p. 161). It therefore stands to reason that Europe is integrating into the already existing, Sinocentric world system. 'This global Sinocentric multilateral trade expanded through the infusion of American money by the Europeans' (1998, p. 126). Whereas Eurocentric bigotry would have it that it was Europe that shaped the world, one may suspect 'that maybe it was the world that made Europe' (1998, p. 3).

As if to make his thesis more convincing, Frank proposes an analogous assessment of the rise of Europe (as NICs, New Industrial Countries) with that of present-day Asia. He writes on this matter: 'The contemporary analogy is that the present world economic crisis permits the rise of what are now called the newly industrialising economies (NIEs) in East Asia … [L]ike these East Asian NIEs now, Europe then engaged first in import substitution (at that time in what was the 'leading' industry of textiles previously imported from Asia) and increasingly also in export promotion – first to their relatively protected markets in West Africa and the Americas and then to the world market as a whole …' (1998, p. 263).

What should therefore be explained, in either case, is the reversal of the position respectively occupied by Europe and Asia – by finding out why Europe usurped Asia's central position (around 1800) and why and how Asia might be able to rehabilitate the latter (at the present time). Frank poses the question: 'The question is how and why beginning around 1800 Europe and then the United States, after long lagging behind, "suddenly" caught up and then overtook Asia economically and politically in the one world economy and system' (1998, p. 284). Frank's answers to this question are vague and fragmented:

> The argument is that it was not Asia's alleged weakness and Europe's alleged strength in the period of early modern world history but rather the effects of Asia's strength that led to its decline after 1750. Analogously, it was Europe's previously marginal position and weakness … that permitted its ascendance after 1800.' (1998, p. 37)

I will return to this formulation enacted like some sort of law of unequal development (of which I propose a version that I think is more convincing). 'The decline of the East preceded the rise of the West' (1998, p. 264). I will specify much later how I would analyse the causes of this 'decline'. 'The Industrial Revolution was an unforeseen event, which took place in a part of Europe as a result of the continuing unequal structure and uneven process in and of the world economy as a whole' (1998, p. 343). I will equally come back to this question, to which the method utilised by Frank does not effectively give room for an answer.

Refusing to recognise the central importance of the turning points in universal history, and therefore the necessary attention to the modern (capitalist) system of production, its new character, qualitatively better than those of all previous systems (both European and Asian of course), Frank is forced to descend to a bland philosophy of history, which has never produced anything new worthy of attention. ('The more things change, the more they remain the same.') Consequently, for Frank, monotonous cycles follow each other. This is all that is possible, once one has the prejudice that nothing of importance can change in the course of history. These cycles are furthermore declared to have been global and never specific to any region of the world.

The same goes with the arguments given to us on the issues of 'hegemonies'. Refusing to read modern history (of 1500 to the present day) as a succession of hegemonies, Frank writes: 'At no time during the four centuries under review was any economy or state able to exercise any significant degree of hegemony, or even leadership, over … the world as a whole' (1998, p. 333). Although I have rejected this particular thesis – popular, it is true, among many authors of the school of the world economy – it is for very strong but different reasons than those cited by Frank.

Frank also asserts that his general theses constitute a condition *sine qua non* for a non-Eurocentric reading of history. Evidently, since his theses are neither those of Marx, nor his bourgeois rivals, nor those of the school of the world economy, nor those of the culture which accompanies the standard Anglo-Saxon economies (we would rather say implicit in the dominant discourses), the combination is possible. Everybody is accused of involvement in the common search for the origins of everything in 'European exceptionalism' (1998, p. 336). With disconcerting nonchalance, Frank almost reduces Marxism to the thesis on the Asiatic mode of production. He writes: 'If several parts of Asia were richer and more productive than Europe [until at least 1750] … how is it possible that the "Asiatic mode of production" could have been as traditional, stationary … as Marx, Weber, Sombart and others alleged?' (1998, p. 35).

The explanations of universal history, alternative to the one that he proposes, would therefore necessarily be Eurocentric in the sense that they affirm that the invention of capitalism could only be the fruit of the European history. It would be an impossible likelihood in China, because of the existence of an imperial state; in India because of the caste system; in the Islamic world because of the inheritance system of nomadic tribalism (see 1998, p. 323–6). From the foregoing, because all analysts of universal history have been Eurocentric bigots, critics of this prejudice are banded together and labelled ideological critics. Frank writes that in their criticism of Eurocentrism, Said, Bernal, Amin, etc 'concentrate on ideological critiques ...' (1998, p. 276).

For me, it will be enough to recall here that I did not, as Frank suggests, wait for Perry Anderson to bury the Asiatic mode of production in 1974 (see 1998, p. 322) before criticising it. Certainly, there have been Marxists who succumbed to Eurocentric prejudice. Perhaps Marx himself was one of them, to some extent, and certainly Perry Anderson, and quite a number of others. But I don't consider myself to be among them. I had buried the Asiatic mode of production already in 1957, while advancing the same arguments very precisely (almost word for word) that Frank uses. I described the theory of this so-called Asiatic mode of production as 'West-centric bigotry' (obviously synonymous with Eurocentric). Furthermore, the interpretation of universal history that I proposed, both in *Class and Nation* and in *Eurocentrism*, is entirely founded on research on the 'general trends' in social evolution. This research aimed at reducing the range[1] of the specifics in space and the time, to insert them in this general trend. The arguments that Frank put together to support his theses – according to which one finds the same forms of social organisation in the Europe of the Middle Ages, the Islamic world, India, or China (for example, trade guilds) were those I advanced at least 30 years ago, but within the framework of another general concept of universal history, the fundamental non-Eurocentric character of which I shall demonstrate further on. My criticisms of Eurocentrism were never restricted to its ideological dimensions. I am surprised that Frank, who read me, did not see this. Should this be the case, it probably is that Frank preferred to throw away the baby with the bath water. Having rejected – rightly so – the Asiatic mode of production, he wanted in the same vein to rule out any debate on modes of production.

I intend, therefore, to expatiate on my analysis of Frank's theses by going to the roots of our divergent views in the pages that follow. I will therefore explain the grounds on which I advance the idea that capitalism and the world capitalist system did bring something new and do not constitute in any way an extension of previous systems. This will make it possible to understand why capitalism produced and will continue to produce polarisation throughout its history, a fact of enormous importance that Frank does not take into consideration in his theses. I will further propose my work on the centuries of mercantilism, a work that, while retaining as true and important many of the 'facts' highlighted by Frank, integrates other fundamental aspects of the reality that the latter chose to ignore here. One will then see that my analysis on the rise of Europe on these conceptual bases has nothing to do with Eurocentrism. I will then examine 'matters for the future'. I will show that the cyclical concept which Frank relies on to analyse the rise of contemporary Asian countries does not make it possible to understand the nature and magnitude of the issues in the conflicts of today and tomorrow. I will conclude by highlighting the dead end in which Frank locks himself in the manner in which he handles the issue of Eurocentrism.

What is new in capitalism and the world capitalist system?

Having shied away from asking himself the questions 'What is capitalism?', 'What is modernity?', Frank takes refuge in a poor conceptualisation of reality, that of the empiricism of conventional economics. Societies are all confronted with the same problems: how to use natural resources and their technological knowledge to produce and trade. It even amounts to the hypothesis of conventional economics. I have already cited an example of this in passing, when Frank speaks of the European and Asian textile industries before 1800. This, of course, had more to do with crafts production and less with manufacturing and industrial production. But for Frank, this is of no importance. The social relations which support these methods of production (crafts or industrial) are more or less of no significance, since they only constitute stages of technological development. For the same basic reason, Frank refuses to see that the capitalist mode of production is not a method of production technologically defined by the use of machines, but a social pattern of organisation that concerns not only production but also social life in all its ramifications. The capitalist mode of production represents a qualitative break with the system that preceded it. The law of value controls not only economic life, but indeed the entire social system of the modern (capitalist) world. It has command over the content of the specific ideology peculiar to this new system ('economism' or better, 'economist alienation'), since it controls the new and specific relationships between the economic base of the system and its ideological and political superstructure (wealth controls power while previously it was power which controlled wealth).[2] This system is, in certain respects, superior, not only because of the prodigious development of the productive forces it has permitted, but also because of its specific function within the political and ideological spectrum (the modern concept of democracy). It is at the same time a system destined by necessity to be surpassed, because the exponential growth that characterises it finds no solution in the framework of its immanent logic. But, as Wallerstein notes, exponential growth is cancerous; it leads invariably to death. Marx's intuitive genius is precisely to have understood that, for this reason, capitalism must be replaced by a qualitatively new system subjecting the development of productive forces to a controlled social logic and no longer to the sole mechanical logic of the alienated economy.

If, as I maintain, in the Marxist tradition, capitalism is defined, first of all, by its specific mode of production, one must await the Industrial Revolution, that is to say, the dominance of big industry founded on the wage-earning class, to speak of the capitalist mode in its finished form.

In preindustrial systems, labour was exploited through the ruling class's control of the access to natural resources, basically land. Since the Industrial Revolution, the type of property that ensures exploitation of labour has shifted to industrial equipment, which therefore became the dominant form of full-fledged capital. That major shift is unseen by Frank and overlooked by those who play down the qualitative change from the mercantilist capitalist transition to full-fledged industrial capitalism. This change has thoroughly modified the patterns of social relations, as well as the relationship between political power and economic laws. The three centuries of European mercantilism (from the Renaissance to 1800) thus constitute only a transition to capitalism, which appears as such only *a posteriori*. One recognises then, *a posteriori*, the ruptures that make it possible to qualify the actual period of transition: the reversal of the preoccupation with the metaphysical peculiar to the tributary ideology, the reinforcement of absolute monarchy founded on the equilibrium of the ancient feudal social forces and of the bourgeoisie, the democratic expression of the English and French revolutions, etc.

I will return much later to this transition. I do not feel, however, any hesitation in qualifying this period as the 'first phase of capitalism'. Marx suggested this in his analysis on 'primitive accumulation', which characterises the centuries others call 'mercantilist'. Whatever the case, 1500 and 1800 then represent the cut-off points of this period.

The modern world not only requires that one conceive the nature of the break that the capitalist mode of production represents. It also requires understanding that the modern system is global. Whether we accept or reject the idea that there had been previous world systems, Frank, Wallerstein, and I (and no doubt many others), all agree that the modern system is global, in the sense that all parts are integrated into the system by virtue of their involvement in the world division of labour, one that involves essential consumer goods whose production runs parallel with a level of commodification incomparable to that obtained in previous periods. Undertaking a more in-depth analysis of this trite evidence, it can be seen that this system takes the form of the world economic system governed by what I would call 'the law of globalised value', which necessarily engenders polarisation and manifestations of pauperisation associated with accumulation at the world level, which is a new phenomenon, without precedent in history. This law governs all the major conflicts which have taken centre stage: those which originate from the revolt of people on the periphery and those between rival groups seeking domination of the global system, determining the efficacy of the various strategies which seek to prevail in the system.

The socialist criticism of capitalism emerged essentially as a criticism of the mode of exploitation of labour by capital. This criticism rose progressively from the plane of moral refusal to that of a more scientific comprehension of the mechanisms and the laws of the system, of its contradictions. However, socialist criticism has remained – historical Marxism included – relatively underdeveloped with respect to the other dimension of capitalism, its spread as a world system. Therefore, the decisive consequences of the polarisation on a worldwide scale has been systematically underestimated. The analyses of capitalism proposed in a global perspective have been instrumental in correcting the inadequacies of historical socialism precisely by pointing out the worldwide character of the capitalist system and its polarising effect on that scale. In that sense, they are irreplaceable. In its immediate expression, the capitalist system appears indeed as a world economy operating in the political framework of a system organised by sovereign states. One must say, however, that the opposition world-economy/world-empire refers necessarily to the qualitative opposition revolving around the capitalist mode of production. In previous modes of production, the laws of the economy do not affirm themselves as autonomous manifestations of necessity, but, on the contrary, as expressions of the ideological and political order. The dominant capitalist centres do not seek to extend their political power through imperial conquest because they can, in fact, exercise their domination through economic means.[3] States of earlier periods did not have the guarantee of the benefits derived from the economic dependency of their possible peripheries as long as the latter remained outside the sphere of their political domination. The theoretical and ideological arguments which have been put forth – most often deliberately as responses to the challenge of socialist criticism of the system, and particularly as responses to Marx – omit the qualitative contrast expressed here, and therefore seek to describe, on countless possible levels of immediate apprehension, specific characteristics of modernity.[4] Such phenomenal analysis flattens history, raises the debate to heights too lofty for abstraction, and, therefore, trivialises the propositions that one may deduce from it.

Be that as it may, the constituent regions (vast empires or modest seigniories) of the tributary world of earlier periods were not necessarily isolated from one another; on the contrary, all historical research corroborates the intensity of their relationships. Nonetheless, the nature of these relationships is different from that which qualifies the connections within the world capitalist system. Certainly, in all cases, it is a question of commercial relationships. But the Marxist critique that insisted on the necessary distinction between the 'market' on the one hand and the 'capitalist market' (in which exchange is based on capitalist production) on the other remains valid. The importance of the market and the intensity of the exchanges, observed here and there through time and space, are not synonymous with capitalism. They indicate only that the replacement of the tributary system – that is to say, the passage to capitalism – had been the order of the day, here and there for a long time, and that the European mercantilist transition is not the product of a specific law of Europe's peculiar evolution, but the expression of a general law of the evolution of all human society.

Pursuing the analysis in terms of mode of production versus world system, as Frank does, is thus not unfounded; on the contrary, these two directions of the analysis are complementary. Nevertheless, having been ambiguously formulated, Frank's analysis in terms of his world system had to lead to a veritable skid, which consists of a reverse extrapolation of the conclusions of the analysis dealing with the capitalist world. The ultimate reason for the misunderstanding is that capitalism cannot be defined by the mere association of three orders of phenomena: private property, wage labour, and the extension of commercial exchanges. This empiricist method conceals the essential reality that capitalism exists only when the level of development of the productive forces involves the modern factory.

It is, in fact, only with capitalism in its finished form, beginning with the Industrial Revolution, that two fundamentals of the modern world appear. The first is the massive urbanisation of society, which leads to qualitative change, since, up until then, all human societies had remained essentially rural. Massive urbanisation needed an agricultural revolution, mechanical and chemical, inconceivable without industry capable of providing its inputs. The second is the henceforth exponential character of the growth of production. The modern world system is a capitalist world system because it is based on capitalism as I have defined it. All past forms of social organisation in all the regions that form part of the modern system are, in turn, subjected to the hegemonic logic of the capitalist system. And this subordinate status of previous original modes is a new phenomenon, unique to world capitalism.

Polarisation is an immanent law of the worldwide expansion of capitalism. This phenomenon is also new in history.[5] Actually existing capitalism, a world phenomenon, is not reducible to the mode of capitalist production and does not intend to become so. For the mode of capitalist production presupposes a three-dimensional integrated market (market of merchandise, capital, and labour) that defines the basis of its functioning. The integration, which was, in fact, constructed in the framework of the history of the formation of the core bourgeois states (Western and Central Europe, the United States and Canada, Japan, Australia) has never been extended to include world capitalism. The world market is exclusively two-dimensional in its expansion, integrating progressively the trade of products and the circulation of capital, to the exclusion of labour whose market remains compartmentalised. I have maintained that this fact was in itself sufficient to engender an inevitable polarisation. In fact, behind the propositions set forth, a poorly expressed theoretical split lay hidden. For some, capitalism was in itself polarising. But, in order to establish this, it was necessary to rise to the level of abstraction defined earlier, namely, the truncated nature of the world market in relationship to the three-dimensional integration peculiar to the capitalist mode of production. For others, such a concrete historical argument fails to establish the general proposition that world capitalism is necessarily polarising. This polarisation was considered phenomenal and non-essential, produced by concrete history and not by the laws of the accumulation of capital.

My proposition defines abstractly world capitalism, just as those concerning the law of value define the capitalist mode of production. Of course, abstraction is not, any more here than elsewhere, a negation of the concrete, but, on the contrary, the expression of the diversity of the latter. The historical conditions that explain the formation of the bourgeois national state at one pole and its absence at the other illustrate the concrete diversity that characterises what I have just called the peripheries.

The definition of the essential content of the two concepts of core and periphery is economic in nature. This is not a question of an arbitrary choice but is the expression of the dominance of economics in the capitalist mode, and of the direct subordination of politics and ideology to the constraints of the accumulation of capital. Consequently, core/periphery relationships are, first of all, economic in nature. On the contrary, if, during earlier periods, phenomena of polarisation are also detectable, they have a different nature and a different dynamic because they operate within the framework of non-capitalist societies.

Polarisation in its modern form appears with the division of the world into industrialised and non-industrialised countries. It is, therefore, a relatively recent phenomenon which constitutes itself in the 19th century. This modern polarisation is still only embryonic and potential at the time of the transition from mercantilism to industrial capitalism – from the 16th to the 18th century. The emergence of the concept of world capitalist polarisation has its own history, of course. Naturally, the debate had opened with concrete and specific considerations, influenced by the period. These considerations stressed an industrial/non-industrial contrast, since polarisation actually expressed itself through it. Industrialisation became thereupon the means of 'development' whose historical objective was supposed to be the abolition of polarisation ('underdevelopment'). Yet, the industrialisation/non-industrialisation contrast is not the eternal and definitive form of capitalist polarisation. Dominant from 1800 to 1945, it becomes blurred little by little after the Second World War with the industrialisation of the peripheries, when the criteria of polarisation shifts to new domains.

Certain ambiguities in the world systems analysis concerning the precise definition of capitalism has led to a skid in the direction of a projection back in time of the characteristics of the modern world. The most extremist view (Frank, for example) goes so far as to claim that the very idea of specificities peculiar to the different modes of production is unfounded, that there is no difference between capitalism and so-called previous systems (in all systems, capitalist and other elements supposedly mingled in the same way), and that the societies of the planet have always been completely integrated in a single world system that dates back to the dawn of time. There they join the long tradition of those philosophies of history that are preoccupied with establishing the eternity of the system and the futility of the efforts to change it. Others, less rash, content themselves with drawing comparisons between the core-periphery relationships at different ages of the evolution, or the cyclical character of the evolution of the systems, or the displacement of the hegemonic centres. No doubt by situating oneself on a high level of abstraction, one will always be able to perceive marked comparisons through the ages. The use of common terminology tends to reinforce the illusion of these analogies. I myself used the terms 'cores' and 'peripheries' in the analyses I proposed for the periods prior to capitalism. I, however, deemed it necessary to specify how the different content of these concepts applied to the varied social systems. I maintain that the amalgam of the periods proceeds from the impoverishment of the concepts.

The recent industrialisation of the peripheries, though unequal, of course, calls for a reconsideration of polarisation, to rid it of its outmoded historical language. Certainly polarisation will continue to be produced by the three-dimensional non-integration of the capitalist market, but it will be within the framework of the system of accumulation at the world level, operating in a world which is tending to become globally industrialised. I have tried to portray, through the analysis of what I call the 'five monopolies', the emerging forms of core–periphery polarisation.

Polarisation produced by global expansion of capitalism in the last two centuries is phenomenal, incomparable to anything ever seen before in terms of unequal development. We are familiar, through the works of Bairoch (and others), to whom Frank refers in fact, that on the eve of the Industrial Revolution, the productivity gap was modest for 80 to 90 per cent of the global population. Had the ratio been 1 to 1.3 or above 1 to 2, or even 1 to 3 in favour of the dynamic regions of Europe over advanced Asia, the magnitude would have still been limited in the opinion of most scholars, including Frank and me. However, these gaps widened fantastically to the ratio of something like 1 to 60 and continue to widen – proof that 1800 is a turning-point in universal history; proof also that capitalism did not fully exist until after the Industrial

Revolution. This phenomenon, new in history, does not seem to bother Frank in the least. Since there is nothing new under the sun, modern polarisation attributed to manifestations of unequal development is old news. Past systems were not polarising by nature; it was possible to 'catch up'. On the contrary, it is no longer the case under capitalism. Frank's blindness on this major issue in modern history will bring him to a fundamentally flawed analyses of the 'miracle' of the NIEs. This blindness keeps him from grasping the real issue in the social conflict of today and tomorrow.

Issues concerning the transition to capitalism

The three centuries of mercantilism, the focus of Frank's work, constitute the most complex period of universal history because the old tributary forms and the emerging new forms of capitalism are associated and operate in both complementary and conflicting manner (perhaps analogous to the ways in which those of capitalism and those of socialism have been functioning in contemporary society). Frank's hypothesis simplifies the interpretation of this phase of history.

To get a clear idea of the nature of the issues and the conflict between the old and the new played out between 1500 and 1800, it is necessary to examine what human societies were like before this conflict and all its implications. I have tried to do this in two ways:

1. By defining, beyond the infinite varieties of local forms, what is common to all ancient societies: the dominance of the politico-ideological power and its expression through the cultures of religious alienation. The concept proposed to this effect (cf. Amin 1980), the tributary society, constitutes the tool for a true non-Eurocentric interpretation of universal history.
2. By proposing a pattern of trade relations between regional partners of this 'world system' (in fact reduced to the Old World – Asia, Europe, Africa) for the duration of 20 centuries which covers the period from the revolutions that created tributary societies (500 to 300 BC) to 1500. The scheme – a similar map to the one proposed by Frank for the period between 1500 to 1800 – brings out the intensity of the trade

among what I call the three tributary centres – Hellenistic, Hindu and Confucian – and the peripheries (Europe, Africa, Japan, Southeast Asia) (Amin 1991; also in Frank and Gills 1993; see also Amin 1996a, ch. 2, p. 69 onwards). Cores and peripheries of this system are not defined in economic terms – through a flashback of capitalism – but in terms of the political and cultural forms of the tributary society.

Is it possible then to describe this system as global? Not quite, since it is not at all parallel to the global character of capitalism. No, not for reasons having to do with the small number of commercial exchanges compared with contemporary trade (a simple quantitative argument), but for fundamental reasons related to the nature of the tributary social system. Based on the dominance of ideology, societies constituted the thriving cultural space and in this way experienced peaceful exchanges and conquest relations that existed between them. A world system would have implied, in their line of thinking, politico-religious unification, an objective that they were not evidently, able to achieve. I prefer to call this kind of relation a system of interconnections between regional systems (corresponding to the cultural spaces in question). Capitalism created a world system of another kind, through the integration of its constituent societies, into a unique economic system, unifying but not homogenising at this level. This unification by itself, in turn, provoked a cultural universalisation without precedent. But this universalism remains truncated, because it is linked to a polarising economic globalisation.

The constitution of the large tributary regions does not lead to their unification in a single state system. On the contrary, the areas defined by the networks of organisation of military and political powers, of economic exchange, of religious and ideological diffusion, do not correspond generally. Their combination, more or less happy, defines different societies, some capable of lasting and blooming, indeed opening up and conquering, others locking themselves into deadly impasses. In this framework, the concept of cores and peripheries and that of hegemony may prove fecund, on condition, however, they are not defined – in comparison to the modern concepts – in terms of economic exploitation. In this framework, the network of exchanges and interactions may permit one to speak of regional systems, on condition also that one does not confuse the highly selective effects of these exchanges with the infinitely more structuring ones of the modern world system, which, for that reason, is the only one that deserves this qualifier.

The reading of history shows, unlike the affirmations of extremists of the (Frankian) world system, the extraordinary durability of the equilibrium of the great poles of the ancient worlds (McNeill 1963; Mann 1986; see also Amin 1996a, p. 98). Durability is not synonymous with static condition. All the ancient systems are, on the contrary, in permanent movement, through the impetus given by a basic identical contradiction that characterises them. This contradiction contrasts the dominant logic of tributary power with the development requirements of productive forces, which is expressed in the tendency towards autonomisation of commercial relations.

The remarkable works of Janet Abu-Lughod (1989), K.N. Chaudhuri (1985), John Fitzpatrick (1991), and G. Coedes (1948),[6] among others, highlight this contradiction in the Islamic Orient, India, and China on all points analogous to that which operated in the European Middle Ages and during the centuries of the capitalist transition. The role of the mercantilist maritime and continental merchant cities of the silk routes, of France, Germany, Italy, the Islamic Orient, Central Asia, Malacca, the Sahara, the East African coast, the seas of China, and Japan is similar everywhere. There is mass production for exportation, but in the framework either of manufactures or the system of handicrafts and the putting-out of products that are not always only prestige items but sometimes everyday items, even if the products are reserved only for the affluent classes.

One can thus speak here of merchant capitalism, as does Marx. The conflict between it, its aspirations to become autonomous in relation to the tributary power, and the maritime expansions it stimulates are not specific to European history. They are found in China, where the transfer of the economic centre of gravity from the 'feudal' north country to the 'maritime' south was on its way to causing the Confucian empire to break up into a constellation of states. Some of these states with a typically mercantile structure could have established in the China Sea or in the Pacific what mercantilism realised later in the Mediterranean and the Atlantic.

The brakes put on by the Mings, like the Turco-Mongolian invasions in the Near East, may, for this reason, appear as accidents of history that gave Europe its chance. Capitalism could have been born here; it is not the product of a European exception to the rule, as suggested by Eurocentric ideology, but on the contrary, it is the normal solution to the fundamental contradiction of all tributary systems. To recognise this fact in no way means, however, that capitalism was already present there, nor that the reason it will appear precisely in that peripheral region of the tributary world – Europe – does not call for a specific analysis of this fact, nor that, consequently, the European mercantilist period contributes nothing new.

All the advanced tributary systems (the Islamic Orient, India, China) were, at the dawn of Europe's conquest of America, agitated by the same basic contradictions that could be surmounted only by the invention of capitalism. The fact remains, nonetheless, that the emergence of this response in Europe must be explained concretely, as the reasons the development of capitalism in Europe arrested the possible evolution in this same direction in other regions of the world, indeed involved them in regressive involutions (Amin, 1980, chs 3, 4).

1. The period 1500–1800 falls under the history of capitalism and not that of European feudalism, even if the capitalism in question was still mercantilist and would emerge in its complete form only with large-scale industry in the 19th century.
2. The European mercantilist transition, in contrast to what developed earlier elsewhere, is singular. This singularity lies in the fact that the absolutist state was not the continuation of the dispersed feudal tributary power of the previous era (which, for that reason, is a peripheral form of the tributary state), but its negation. Whereas, elsewhere (in the Islamic Orient, India, and China), the tributary state assumed from the beginning its mature form (which I call central) and maintained it.
3. During the phase 1150–1300, European feudalism underwent an expansion subjected to its own internal logic, through the clearing of new lands. This expansion was exhausted during the following phase (1300–1450), marked by decreasing

productivity; but the political system remained unchanged (feudal). These two phases are thus of a completely different nature from those of the subsequent phases of capitalist expansion and crisis. The peripheral character of the European tributary formation reveals a flexibility that may be contrasted with the relative rigidity of the advanced central tributary forms: the crisis of the feudal system was surmounted by the emergence of the absolutist state which, by means of the conquest of America, created a mercantilist world economy in whose service it placed itself.

4. The concept according to which the absolutist state must be feudal in nature, because, by its very essence, the capitalist state must be liberal, is a deformation produced by bourgeois ideology which has, moreover, produced other confusions. For example, that Great Britain's advantage over its principal rival, France, would be said to have stemmed from its political system (the beginnings of liberalism in the 18th century) or from its ideology (Protestantism) or from technological superiority. In reality, this advantage is basically the result of Great Britain's privileged position in the system of exploitation of the American peripheries.

5. The establishment of a new system of core–periphery relations between Atlantic Europe and America is not the repetition of the extension of trade in the earlier periods. America does not 'trade' with Europe; it is moulded to be integrated as a periphery economically exploited by mercantilist Europe. Among the authors of the world system school, J.M. Blaut (1989, 1991; Amin 1990) emphasises, correctly, the extraordinary importance of this exploitation, which found expression in, among others: a considerable flux of gold and silver, reinforcing the social position of the new merchant capitalists in European society and giving them a decisive advantage over their competitors (they could offer better prices worldwide); and secondly, in a huge volume of profits drawn from the American plantations. In 1600 the exports of sugar from Brazil represent twice the total exports of England.

6. The two cycles, of expansion (1450–1600) then of readjustment (1600–1750), of the mercantilist world economy, have

their own nature, different in essence from that of the later cycles of full-fledged capitalism.

7. In the birth of European capitalism, two factors (the flexibility of the feudal peripheral tributary mode, the construction of a mercantilist world economy and the moulding of the Americas into this framework) are thus indissolubly linked. I have contrasted this analysis, which I have described as 'unequal development' (the qualitative forward leap emerges from the peripheries of the earlier system) with the culturalist arguments about the 'European miracle', dominant throughout the Eurocentric deformation of Western ideology (recourse to the mythical Greek ancestor, Christianophilia, racism).

8. The capitalist character of the mercantilist transition expresses itself in the ideological rupture that accompanies the formation of the absolutist state: abandonment of the metaphysical hegemony.

The examination of the transition period from 1500 to 1800 that I propose is very different from that of Frank. I view this period as characterised by a major new conflict. On the one hand, there is the power which will install the modern system, that is to say a hierarchised economic system, centred on Europe (expanded to the United States and later Japan, which constitute the contemporary 'Triad' imposing on the rest of the world (the majority) the status of peripheral victims of a wholesale and unprecedented polarisation. At the other pole are forces that resist the dismantling of the old systems in all their ramifications (but end up losing the war) that is to say, at the level of the local organisation, as well as at the corresponding levels of regional and international systems.

The differences between the old and new systems, which Frank does not recognise, are vast. In the old system, the majority of the population of the globe was concentrated at the core: in the new, the core is the minority. In the old system, the three centres enjoyed considerable autonomy, unrelated to the high level of interdependence among the modern Triad. Without recalling once again the polarisation proper to capitalism, the old system allowed room to catch up. The proof is that peripheral Europe was able to catch up in a very short time. The modern system

makes it impossible to make up for lost ground within the framework of its logic of production.

I therefore consider the period 1500–1800 as that of conflict
between the two systems. The map which Frank proposes in his
work illustrates the complementary conflict combination of the
corresponding network of the new project of capitalism centred
on Europe (and later the Triad) and networks inherited from
the past (which constitute the sub-systems in East Asia and the
Indian Ocean). The old sub-systems were progressively losing
their autonomy, either to be destroyed or subdued by the new
capitalist network.

I say progressively because Asia, in many ways, remained
more advanced than Europe before the latter began its conquest
of the world. On this score, I have no bones to pick with the
arguments raised by Frank. On the contrary, they were those I
have been advancing for a long time. But I do not interpret them,
as does Frank, that 'nothing has changed'. If Asia lost this war
and if Europe won, this calls for reflection and explanation. The
explanation Frank advances on this subject is poor: Europe benefited from the Asian crisis. Which crisis? And why did Asia not
overcome (the crisis) by its own means? With regard to China, the
work of Jean Chesneaux and Marianne Bastid (1969) propose the
best analysis of the crisis in question:

> The relationship between population and economic activity,
> relationship which was favourable up to the middle of the
> eighteenth century, was overturned toward 1780–1800. It was a
> change in which the combination of population and economic
> growth gave way to crisis, and the depletion of resources in
> relation to the needs of a population which continued to
> expand rapidly. (1969, p. 43)

One is forced to agree with Chesneaux and Bastid that none of the
succeeding Chinese systems, neither those of the empire nor that
of the Kuomintang republic, were able to overcome this crisis, and
China had to wait for the Communist revolution to witness the
beginning of its resolution. I do not think it would be possible to
explain the resistance of Chinese society to the qualitative transformation of its organisation (which was required to overcome

the crisis) without considering the extraordinary rigidity of an advanced full-fledged tributary system, the case in China. I compare this rigidity of central societies to the flexibility of the peripheral modes, and come up with the hypotheses of unequal development in history of a fundamentally non-Eurocentric nature. In this sense, China was not more 'traditionalist' than Europe in the past as Frank would have it; it has become so. Europe, being peripheral, suddenly became more flexible, more open to change. To have noted this does not amount to Eurocentrism. Eurocentrism exists when one explains this flexibility by immanent virtues unique to Europe; it is not the case when one explains it through general laws functioning in all human societies.

In this sense, also, it sounds excessive to say that during the mercantile period nothing new was invented. No doubt, Europe did not invent much which was not known elsewhere before the 19th century, in the domain of technology and the organisation of trade. But Europe was able to invent new things in other domains, such as the organisation of power and relations to economic life. Europe was, therefore, the first to invent capitalism – which, I said, could well have originated elsewhere. This is not nothing. Having deliberately removed from his research concerns everything that has to do with politics and ideology, social relations and social issues, everything that is outside economics, Frank refuses to see the magnitude of the changes in question.

I would add that it is necessary to take another look at most of the things he writes about Asia. In my analysis concerning past systems (from 500 BC to 1500 AD), I thought it useful to lay emphasis on the particularities proper to the evolution of each of the three major central areas. China experienced practically continuous development from its beginning to the middle of the 18th century, which gave it a stable advance over all other societies and a force which explains why it managed to escape colonisation, even after its defeat during the second half of the 19th century. The quasi-regular growth of its population and its expansion to the south of the Yangtze (the figures which Frank gave on this subject are the same as mine) bear testimony to this dynamism (which is contrary to the Eurocentric debate on an Asian 'stagnation' that was said to be unparalleled for two millennia). One then begins to appreciate the admiration shown China by the Europeans (which

I highlighted; see Etiemble 1988). The development of India (here also my figures are not different from Frank's), was more chaotic and ran into crisis much earlier. This probably explains the ease with which India was conquered by Dupleix and then the British. The case of the Middle East centre was much more doubtful. Frank, like me, observes that the population of the region has remained practically stagnant for nearly two millennia, up to the 19th century. The techniques of production in agriculture and crafts equally recorded very little evolution. One can therefore speak of stagnation rather than of continuous development. And if the region appeared 'brilliant' in comparison to peripheral Europe up to the 14th century, it is simply inherited from its more prestigious past. Up to the first century of our era, the region had been the most advanced on the planet, even ahead of China and India. But neither the Byzantine empire nor the Arab Caliphate, neither the Ottoman nor the Persian empires, achieved serious progress beyond what had been attained much earlier.

The future: end of the cycle or new invention?

Frank has therefore given up the effort to locate and explain in universal history those qualitative changes which make successive phases different from one another, whether at local levels or at that of the global system. Instead, he substitutes a monotonous cyclical vision of an eternal beginning based on a kind of far-fetched popular philosophy.

The last two centuries have been those of Euro-American hegemony. Today, Asia is 'climbing'; why would the region not revert tomorrow to what it was in the past, the centre of the world? One has lost count of the journalistic articles and books that have come up with this type of 'prediction' without conducting a thorough analysis of the real challenges facing contemporary society. And like many people, the media which have made a name in this genre, have never asked the question of the future of capitalism – which for them is evidence of eternity ('the end of history'). Asia would simply replace Europe within the context of this eternal logic. Frank's thesis says nothing more, alas.

Furthermore, since, according to Frank, the system has always been global and identical, the last cycle, which is on its way out, is not different from the preceding ones, perhaps dating back before 1800 or even 1500. Besides, all these cycles were of necessity global, because herein lies the only real quality of the system, according to Frank. I must say none of the arguments Frank and others – who rather too easily adopted the idea of the 'long cycle' (many of them are among the authors of global economy and related issues) – have convinced me of the evidence of these 'cycles'. One of their arguments, strong in appearance, is the Black Plague, which hit Asia and Europe and affected the population dynamics in a slightly general way. I would say that this incident has no relationship with our subject. The spread of the Black Plague only goes to prove that the earth is round, that human beings are animals, all of whom are prone to the same diseases, that the links between the regions of the world ensure such a transmission. This fact does not prove in any way that the links between the regions of the world are of the same nature in the past as they are at present.

In contrast with the eternal vision of the eternal commencement of the cyclic world (even if it were inscribed in a general movement of productive forces), the method that I recommend is founded on the distinction between the eventual cycles (without prior prejudice to their existence) in the modern capitalist system (after 1800), in its inception phase (from 1500 to 1800), and during the previous tributary era (before 1500). No social or even natural phenomenon develops in a regular, continuous, and indefinite manner. The same is true, perforce of capitalist expansion, whose phases of rapid growth are necessarily followed by difficult moments of readjustment. These phases give the reader of the historical series describing the phenomenon the impression of a long wave evolution. Nonetheless, to recognise the succession of phases is not necessarily to admit a cyclical theory. For, if words have meaning, one can speak of a cycle only if these are definite mechanisms that monotonously reproduce its movement. It is necessary that the articulation of the different dimensions of reality (economic flux, technological innovations, social and political conflicts, etc) function in an identical manner from one cycle to the other. Adherence to the principle according to which capitalism must be analysed as a world system in no way implies the principle that capitalist expansion would be subjected to a law of cyclical development.

The analysis of the economic dimension proper finds, in capitalism, its specific justification stemming from the fact that the system is controlled in its totality directly by the laws of its economic development. But it is important to define precisely the nature of the economic laws in question, the duration (short or long) of their deployment. One then obtains a better grasp of the relativity of the autonomy of economics; that is to say, the limits imposed upon it by the integration between the deployment of its laws, on the one hand, and the reactions they provoke in the social milieu in which they operate, on the other.

One can without great difficulty construct an autogenous economic model of a monotonous cycle by bringing into play the two known mechanisms of the 'multiplier' and of the 'accelerator'. One can improve the model by grafting onto it a cycle of the responses of credit and of the relative variations of real wages and the rate of profit. One can expose this model in the framework of a closed or open national economy, or in that of the world economy. All these economic exercises are conceived in the rigorous abstract framework of the capitalist mode of production, a necessary and sufficient condition of their validity. It is interesting to note that the results obtained by this means describe accurately the actual framework of the short cycle (seven years on the average) that marks out, in fact, the long century, 1815–1945. After the Second World War, a more pronounced degree of control of the economy seems to have been imposed, through mechanisms such as the more active intervention of the state, credit control, income distribution and public expenditures.

Reflection upon the more profound tendencies of the capitalist economic system is the object of controversies. Theories concerning the long cycles (so-called Kondratieff cycles) are situated on this plane.[7] Here, I share with a few others, a minority thesis, which is totally ignored by conventional economics, by the analysis of the world-system school (who all, it seems to me, admit the long cycle), and by the dominant Marxist currents. The thesis I am defending is founded on the idea that the capitalist mode of production expresses an inherent social contradiction, which has lead in turn to a permanent tendency of the system to produce more that can be consumed: pressure on wages tends to generate a volume of profits, saved and earmarked for investment by the competition, which is always relatively too big in comparison with the investments necessary to meet the final demand. The threat of relative stagnation is, from that angle, the chronic illness of capitalism. It is not the crisis that must be explained by specific reasons but, rather, the peculiar expansion that is the product of circumstances specific to each of its phases (Amin 1996a; Foster 1986). I contend that this contradiction is inherent to the capitalist mode of production in the full sense of the word; that is to say, once again realised through modern industry. I am certainly not proposing to project this specific law back in time, either to ancient times, or even to the transition of mercantilist capitalism (1500–1800). There is no tendency toward overproduction, in any society, prior to modern capitalism.

In the framework of this fundamental theory of the capitalist mode of production, the discussion of the apparent cycles takes a turn quite different from that produced by the world-system school. Each of the growth phases (successively 1790–1814, 1848–72, 1893–1914, 1945–68) do not only have their own unique character, but also are set in motion by mechanisms which are not cyclical, in the sense that they are different in nature from one phase to the other. I refer the reader to what I wrote previously on this subject. I would add that the backward projection, before 1800 and all the more so before 1500, of a cycle implies even more disastrous amalgams and a vulgar reduction of the concept of relations between the economic base and the political and ideological superstructure.

The succession of hegemonies is generally associated with the reading of long cycles of universal history (Amin 1996a, pp. 91–4). The least one can say is that the rivalry of political formations is a reality just as permanent in history as the social conflicts inside these formations. The truth of this statement is such that, in contrast to Marx's affirmation, according to which history was above all the history of the class struggle, some have proclaimed that history was above all the struggle of nations. Is it possible to build a bridge between these two apparently mutually exclusive affirmations?

Historians have always come up against the difficulties of this task. According to some, the history of capitalism – from 1500 onwards, perhaps from 1350 – should be reread as that of a succession of hegemonies exercised by a particular power over the capitalist world economy. In a general way, the thesis of the world system tipped the scales too much in the direction its automatic option demanded; that is, the determination of the parts, the states, by the whole, the world economy. I prefer – like Szentes (1985) – to place the emphasis on the dialectic of contradiction between the internal (national) and the external (world system) forces. This attitude leads one immediately to qualify strongly the proposed responses to the question of hegemonies. First of all, of course, the would-be hegemony in the capitalist world economy was not a world hegemony. The world was not reduced from the 16th to the 19th century to Europe and its American appendix. Saying Venice or the United Provinces were 'hegemonic' means nothing on the actual scale of the time. But even on the European capitalist world-economy scale, I do not see how one can call Venice or the United Provinces hegemonic. They were remarkable financial and commercial centres, for sure, but, indeed, constrained to reckon with the rural feudal world that hemmed them in on all sides and with the political balances that it involved throughout the conflicts of the great monarchies. The treaty of Westphalia, in 1648, did not consecrate a Dutch hegemony, but a European equilibrium that annulled it. I contest even that one may speak of a British hegemony in the 18th century. Great Britain conquered advantageous positions on the seas at the time, to the detriment of its French rival. But it was neither capable yet of affirming a distinct power in the affairs of the European continent, nor even of really dominating the potential overseas peripheries. Its hegemony would not be acquired until quite late, after China and the Ottoman empire were 'opened' (beginning in 1840), and after the revolt of the Sepoys in India was put down (1857). The industrial advancement and the financial monopoly of Great Britain, real at the time, led to no true hegemony. Indeed, to make industrial production the key world economic activity required rather a European equilibrium, and therefore that Great Britain did not dominate. In reality, the situation was such that scarcely had the hegemony of Great Britain been constituted (from 1850 to 1860) then it was challenged by the rise of its competitors, Germany and the United States, even though London maintained a privileged financial position.

Hegemony, far from constituting the rule in the history of world capitalist expansion, is rather the exception, of short and fragile duration. The law of the system is, rather, that of durable rivalry. Have things changed since? Or are they on the way to changing really? In certain aspects, the hegemony of the United States after 1945 is, in fact, actually of a new character. The United States has, for the first time in the history of humanity, military means of intervention (be it by destruction or by genocide) of planetary dimensions. Limited from 1945 to 1990 by the military bipolarity shared with the former Soviet Union, the United States has perhaps become what before it none had been, except Hitler in his imagination: the (military) master of the world.... But for how long?

Back to the issue of the rise of contemporary Asia, I would say it is far from assuming the magnitude visualised by popular literature. In this debate I placed emphasis on what I called the 'five monopolies' which in the foreseeable future would reinforce the powers of the Triad in its overall relations with the modern peripheries, including those on the road to rapid development (in Asia and elsewhere). These monopolies reinforce the Triad's world hegemony through technological initiative, control of financial flows, access to the natural resources of the planet, communications and media, and weapons of mass destruction.

These five monopolies, taken as a whole, define the framework within which the law of globalised value operates. The law of value is the condensed expression of all these conditions, and not the expression of objective, pure, economic rationality. The conditioning of all of these processes annuls the impact of industrialisation in the peripheries, devalues the latter's productive work, and overestimates the supposed value added from the activities of the new monopolies from which the cores profit. What results is a new hierarchy, more unequal than ever before, in the distribution of income on a world scale, subordinating the industries of the peripheries and reducing them to the role of subcontracting. This is the new foundation of polarisation, presaging its future forms.

The crisis which has hit East and Southeast Asia[8] confirms how important these monopolies had become. The dominant transnational capital may succeed through its intervention during the crisis, in organising the countries of Southeast Asia. In spite of appearances, they have in no way outgrown the stage of peripheral industrial economies ('Ersatz-capitalism'). The scenario is completely different with regard to Korea, the exception among contemporary Third World countries, and the only one among them which has succeeded in constructing the core model of a new capitalist economy. It is no surprise that the ongoing financial crisis should be an opportunity for the diplomacy of Washington and its Japanese and European allies to try to dismantle Korea's potential. The financial crisis facing Korea is minor, in the sense that France and Great Britain, for example, have encountered about ten of these crises in the post-war decades without prompting the powers in Washington to propose what they are trying to impose on Korea today. It is minor in the sense that Korea's current external deficit, measured in relation to GDP for example, and in terms of length of time, is smaller than that of the United States. However, what does one find? The IMF simply attributes the existence of the crisis to monopolies in Korea (as if the big American, Japanese, and European companies were not part of it all) and proposes that they be dismantled and the most juicy pieces allocated to American monopolies. One would therefore expect that the IMF would, in order to resolve the American problem, make a similar proposal for the sell-off of Boeing (which is a monopoly as far as I know), for example, to Airbus, its European rival (which is also a monopoly). Mr Camdessus, despite his French nationality, would be recalled by order of President Clinton in the next hour if he dared make such a preposterous proposal! Should one therefore be surprised if the Korean press does not hesitate in talking about the new Korean war, with fingers pointing at Washington as the aggressor? This war, in my opinion, is bound to be drawn out. There will be ups and downs, no doubt, but it is not certain that the United States and its allies will emerge victorious.

Behind Korea is China, whose evolution will certainly weigh even more heavily on the future of the world system. I have suggested elsewhere several possible scenarios concerning this evolution, which largely depend on those internal factors which Frank deliberately chooses to ignore (Amin 1996a, ch. 7, p. 225 onwards; Amin 1998, p. 133–44).

The impending long war has already begun on the terrain of

financial globalisation, which has been rejected by China, India and probably Korea, carrying along with them other countries in South Asia and perhaps elsewhere in Latin America. If this first battle is won, it will be possible to go beyond the attempt by the G7 to limit the damage by instituting regulatory global mechanisms that would enable the ruling transnational capital to remain the master of the game. Henceforth, other battles will be waged in their turn, in what I have described as the long transition to world socialism. The future remains open and will not allow itself to be locked up in the mechanical mould of the cycle imagined by Frank.

The real stakes in the fight to come cannot be reduced to the positions that the Triad and others (the NIEs of Asia and Latin America) will occupy in the capitalist system of tomorrow. The polarisation inherent to world capitalism, deliberately ignored by the would-be liberal ideology, renders these ideological propositions meaningless. Integration into the world system creates, in fact, an insurmountable contradiction in the framework of the logic of the expansion of capital. It makes illusory every attempt of the peripheries, whose peoples represent at least three-fourths of humanity, to 'catch up', that is to say, to assure its peoples a standard of living comparable to those of the privileged minority of the core.

Liberal ideology would have meaning only if it dared to proclaim the total abolition of borders, to open them to migrations of workers as it calls for opening them to trade and to the flow of capital. Then, actually, the ideology would be consistent, and proposing by means of capitalism to achieve the homogenisation of social conditions on a worldwide scale. This opening is not on the agenda. The defenders of liberal ideology will say that opening the borders to trade and to the flow of capital is second best. Under these limited conditions it is the cause of unacceptable polarisation. One might as well say that death is second best after life! Liberal ideology is thus pure trickery, for the real second best must be defined on the basis of the criterion of its capacity to reduce polarisation. In this spirit, logic holds that if migratory flows must be controlled, the opening to trade and to the flow of capital must be as well. That is why 'delinking' defines an essential condition for a gradual reduction of polarisation.

The thesis, according to which no society can escape the permanent challenge of the worldwide expansion of capitalism (and therefore that 'development' is nothing more than development within this system), that there is no autonomous development possible outside of it, is mere recognition of the actual fact but immediately surrenders the possibility that it is possible to change the world. It is necessary to distinguish capitalist expansion and development and not confuse the two concepts, even if in everyday usage the confusion is, alas, frequent. Capitalist expansion is, by nature, polarising. Development must be, by definition, of a different nature so as to overcome this polarisation. The concept of development is in essence a critical concept.

The ideology of development that dominated the scene after the Second World War did not make this distinction clearly. For some, the national Third World bourgeoisie, the objective of development was to catch up by means of appropriate state policies while remaining in the world system. For others, the so-called socialist states, this same objective (to catch up) which implies some obvious similarities, was mixed with shreds of the contradictory objective of building 'another society'. Furthermore, the uncontrollable exponential growth produced by the logic of the capitalist mode of production is, as ecologists have rediscovered, suicidal. Capitalism, at once as mode of production and world system, is thus simultaneously globally suicidal and criminal with respect to the peoples. The world has been launched into a new phase of history which Frank's method does not even allow one to suspect. A long phase of transition from world capitalism to world socialism, similar to the long transition from 1500 to 1800, is characterised by the action of both complementary and contradictory forces, some continuing to act in the logic of the reproduction of social relations proper to capitalism, and some imposing another social logic still to be invented (Amin 1996b, pp. 244–58; Amin 1996a, p. 309 onwards).

Final considerations concerning Eurocentrism

Eurocentrism is a form of what I would generally call culturalism. By this I mean that there are transhistoric invariables among 'cultures' proper to various peoples. In the particular case of

Eurocentrism, there are various versions of this affirmation, attributing 'the European genius' either to the Greek ancestor (European civilisation had carried with it, according to the Greeks, a Promethean sense and/or the concept of democracy), or 'the genius of Christianity' of the so-called Judeo-Christian tradition, or the more popular genes of the 'race'. In all cases, I found mythologies manufactured in modern times to legitimise European domination of the world capitalist system. Ancient Greeks had nothing to do with the Europe of that time, it was a periphery in the system of the era. Greece interacted with Egypt, Mesopotamia, Iran, one of the constituent elements of the Middle Eastern centre. Hellenism, Christianity and Islam were the successive forms of this tributary construction. As for Christianity, it was first a philosophy reflecting the real alienation of the tributary system before being constrained by the external capitalist transformation to adjust to the new demands of modern society. I would equally add that the link Judaism–Islam is certainly stronger than that which has characterised Judeo-Christian continuity. Eurocentrism is thus in effect an ideology that enables its defenders to conclude that 'modernity' (or/and capitalism) could only have been born in Europe, which subsequently offered it to other peoples ('the civilising mission').

The mode of today is culturalism. There are, in fact, other declarations of a similar nature, which emanate as reactions to Eurocentrism. Islamists, Hinduists, adherents of Africanity or Asian specificity, indigenists of all kinds are found everywhere and equally assume that there are in their 'cultures' transhistorical invariables which are superior to those of the glorified Eurocentric West. 'Yes, we are fundamentally different from one another', they say. This is why I call these culturalisms reverse Eurocentrisms. Besides, each and every one agrees to submit to the same rigors of capitalism. The manipulation of culturalisms is therefore not difficult to set in motion, should the need arise.

I have categorically rejected the culturalist argument. The cultures, including the religions, can transform themselves, can adjust to, or can resist the demands of the times, then perish and disappear from the scene. I have always sought to develop conceptual systems which make it possible to understand that history is universal, that it is not constituted by juxtaposed segments which are irreducible one to the other. Concrete specificity – which continues to exist (each society and each given time in history has its specificities) – explains the universality of 'laws' (if they are referred to as such) which regulate social life. This is the reason why I criticised the so-called Asiatic mode of production already in 1957. It is this concern for universalism that has led me to propose the family of communal modes of production, and that of the tributary family, as constituent elements common to all pre-capitalist societies, and therefrom, the infinite variety of both those forms.

Because the same contradictions are characteristic of all tributary societies, the latter could not overcome them except by inventing capitalism; and this invention was on the current agenda in the entire tributary world, not only in Europe. But Europe had been faster than others and for a long time more advanced. Why? It is in response to this question that I introduced the concepts of the (full-fledged) central tributary mode and the (incomplete) peripheral tributary mode. Feudalism is, in this analysis, a peripheral mode, derived from offshoots of communal systems of the barbarians of the Roman tributary system. This peripheral character manifested itself through the splitting of the power system which characterised feudalism, distinct from its marked centralisation in the complete mode. On the other hand, the 'backwardness' in the European tributary formation explains the specification of absolute monarchy which was constituted only in the modern epoch, in concomitance with mercantilism. In other words, being peripheral, the European tributary model (feudalism) proved more flexible, favouring the same acceleration of historical evolution. This reading of comparative history has nothing to do with either Greek ancestors or with Christianity (be it the one reserved for Protestantism as in Weber), but is based on exclusively universal concepts. It explains the particular through the general. It is fundamentally nonculturalist, non-Eurocentric.

Capitalism is not a more advanced technological level, nor a mode of production strictly defined. It is, like every other society, a whole in which the facets are multiple. Capitalism has therefore produced a culture, its culture, just as the tributary system produced its own. That I use the singular here –the tributary system, the tributary culture – is meant to emphasise that, beyond the variety of their forms of expression, these cultures share basic identical characteristics, which I have described as tributary alienation. In the same way, the culture of capitalism is defined by its own form of alienation, mercantilist alienation. 'Moneytheism' has replaced monotheism. The 'market' rules like the ancient God. I am therefore talking about the capitalist culture and refuse to be drawn into the pervasive vulgar definition of 'Western culture', joint product of Eurocentric affirmation for some (the winners of the system) and thereafter reverse Eurocentrism (the losers).

If this is the case, if there is a problem, it is because capitalist expansion has always been, and remains, polarising. As a result, the universal culture that it proposes is also truncated. There is no conflict of cultures. Behind its eventual appearance hovers the real conflict, that of societies. In this perspective, modernity cannot be rejected in the illusory prospect of a return to the past. On the contrary, it is necessary to pursue development, put an end to its truncated character. But for this, it is necessary to go beyond capitalism. In other words, to seriously fight Eurocentrism, which has kept company with the polarising character of capitalist expansion, one should admit that the transformation of history is possible, that the invention of the new is necessary, something that Frank does not want to imagine. Failing that, modern societies will continue to become entangled in obscure battles which lead nowhere other than the self-destruction of humanity.

This chapter is an edited version of a paper that was first published in 1999 as 'History conceived as an eternal cycle', Review, *vol. XXII, no. 3, pp. 291–326.*

Notes

1. Amin (1980, chs 3 and 4, pp. 46–103) and Amin (1989). The reader will find in these books my views with respect to the central and peripheral forms of tributary mode of production, unequal development throughout history, as well as a critique of Eurocentric culturalism. The conclusions of those analyses are briefly summarised in the following pages. See also Amin and Frank (1978).
2. See my views on the conceptualisation of the social systems and capitalism by Karl Marx, Braudel and Polanyi in Amin (1996b).
3. On the question of 'territorialism' (the tendency to establish large areas governed as single political unit), see Amin (1996b, pp. 235–38).

4. See my critique of Weber's German parochialism in Amin (1996a) and Amin (1992).

5. Amin (1997, ch. 1, 'The future of global polarisation', 1–11). This is an analysis of the 'five monopolies' which operate to the benefit of the Triad and tend to reproduce a deepened polarisation, in spite of the industrialisation of the peripheries. See also: the analysis of the relation between the active and the passive labour army, the debates on the semiperipheries, Amin (1996a, pp. 79, 82-4); the debates on the phases of financialisation of capital, in industrial capitalism and in the mercantilist transition, Amin (1996b, pp. 238–44).

6. See also some examples of misprojection of theses of the world economy into periods prior to 1500 AD in Amin (1996a, pp. 101–02).

7. See my comments on long waves in Amin (1996a, pp. 88–91). I certainly do not mind calling them 'Kondratieff waves', or A-phases of expansion and B-phases of crisis and adjustment in capitalist production. Beyond semantics, I discuss the nature of those cycles.

8. This chapter was first published in 1999 so the Asian crisis referred to is that of the 1990s.

References

Abu-Lughod, Janet (1989) *Before European Hegemony: The World System AD 1250–1350*, Oxford and New York, NY, Oxford University Press

Amin, Samir (1980) *Class and Nation, Historically and in the Current Crisis*, New York, NY, Monthly Review Press

——(1989) *Eurocentrism*, New York, NY, Monthly Review Press

——(1990) 'Colonialism and the rise of capitalisms: a comment', *Science and Society*, vol. 64, no. 1, pp. 67–72

——(1991) 'The ancient world system versus the modern capitalist world system', *Review*, vol. 14, no. 3, pp. 349–85

——(1992) 'Capitalisme et système-monde', *Sociologie et Societes*, vol. 24, no. 2, pp. 181–202

——(1996a) *Les défis de la mondialisation*, Paris, L'Harmattan

——(1996b) 'The challenge of globalisation', *Review of International Political Economy (RIPE)*, vol. 3, no. 2, pp. 216–59

——(1997) *Capitalism in the Age of Globalization: The Management of Contemporary Society*, London, Zed Books

——(1998) *The Future of Maoism* (augmented edn), Delhi, Rainbow

Amin, Samir and Frank, André Gunder (1978) *L'accumulation dependante*, Paris, Anthropos

Blaut, James M. (1989) 'Colonialism and the rise of capitalism', *Science and Society*, vol. 53, no. 3, pp. 260–96

——(1991) 'Fourteen Ninety-Two', unpublished

Chaudhuri, K. N. (1985) *Trade and Civilisation in the Indian Ocean: An Economic History from the Rise of Islam to 1750*, Cambridge and New York, NY, Cambridge University Press

Chesneaux, Jean and Bastid, Marianne (1969) *La Chine, I: Des guerres de l'opium a la guerre francochinoise, 1840–1885*, Paris, Hatier

Coedes, George (1948) *Les états hindouises d'Indochine et d'Indonesie*, Paris, de Boccard

Etiemble, René (c. 1988) *L'Europe chinoise*, Paris, Gallimard

Fitzpatrick, John W. (1991) *Wars, States and Markets in North East Asia, 800–1400 AD*, Vancouver, ISA

Foster, John Bellamy (1986) *The Theory of Monopoly Capitalism*, New York, NY, Monthly Review Press

Frank, André Gunder (1998) *ReORIENT: Global Economy in the Asian Age*, Berkeley, CA, University of California Press

Frank, André Gunder and Gills, Barry K. (eds) (1993) *The World System: Five Hundred Years or Five Thousand?* London, Routledge

Mann, Michael (1986) *The Sources of Social Power, I: to 1760*, Cambridge and New York, NY, Cambridge University Press

McNeill, William H. (1963) *The Rise of the West: A History of the Human Community*, Chicago, IL, University of Chicago Press

Szentes, Tamas (1985) *Theories of World Capitalist Economy*, Budapest, Akademiaikiado

Wallerstein, Immanuel (1997) 'Merchant, Dutch, or historical capitalism?', *Review*, vol. 20, no. 2, pp. 243–54

 5

Europe and China: two paths of historical development

The general and the particular in the trajectories of humanity's evolution

The concrete, the immediate, is always particular – this is virtually a truism. To stop there would make it impossible to understand the history of humanity. This seems – at the phenomenal level – as if it were composed of a succession of particular trajectories and evolutions, without any connections with each other, except by chance. Each of these successions can only be explained by particular causalities and sequences of events. This method reinforces the tendency towards 'culturalisms'; that is, the idea that each 'people' is identified by the specifics of its 'culture', which are mostly 'transhistoric', in the sense that they persist in spite of change.

Marx is, for me, the key thinker on research into the general, as it goes beyond the particular. Of course the general cannot be announced *a priori* through reflection and idealised reasoning about the essence of phenomena (as Hegel and Auguste Comte would do). It must be inferred from analysis of concrete facts. In such conditions it is clear that there is no 'absolute' guarantee that the proposed induction will be definitive, or even accurate. But such research is obligatory: it cannot be avoided.

When you analyse the particular you will discover how the general makes itself felt through forms of the particular. That is how I read Marx.

With this in mind, I have proposed a reading of historical materialism based on the general succession of three important stages in the evolution of human societies: the community stage, the tributary stage and the capitalist stage (potentially overtaken by communism). And I have tried, within this framework, to see in the diversity of the societies at the tributary stage (as in the previous community stage), the particular forms of expression of the general requirements that define each of these stages (see my book *Class and Nation*). The proposition goes against the tradition of a banal opposition between the 'European path' (that of the famous five stages – primitive communism, slavery, feudalism, capitalism and socialism, which was not an invention of Stalin but the dominant view in Europe before and after Marx) and the so-called Asiatic path (or, rather, impasse). The hydraulic thesis, as proposed by Wittfogel, then seemed to me overly infantile and mistaken, based on Eurocentric prejudices. My proposition also goes against another tradition, produced by vulgar Marxism, that of the universality of the five stages.

With this also in mind, I proposed looking at the contradictions within the large family of the tributary societies as expressions of a general requirement to go beyond the basic principles of the organisation of a tributary social system by the invention of those that define capitalist modernity (and, beyond, the possibility of socialism/communism). Capitalism was not destined to be Europe's exclusive invention. It was also in the process of developing in the tributary countries of the East, particularly in China, as we shall see later. In my early critique of Eurocentrism, I brought up this very question, which had been ejected from the dominant debate by the discourse on the 'European exception'.

However, once capitalism was constituted in its historic form, that is, starting from Europe, its worldwide expansion through conquest and the submission of other societies to the requirements of its polarising reproduction put an end to the possibility of 'another path' for the capitalist development of humanity (the 'Chinese path' for example). This expansion destroyed the impact and importance of the variations of local capitalisms and involved them all in the dichotomy of the contrast between the dominant capitalist/imperialist centres with the dominated capitalist peripheries, which defines the polarisation peculiar to historical capitalism (European in origin).

I am therefore now proposing a reading of the 'two paths' (that of Mediterranean/Europe and that of the Chinese world), which is not that of the opposition five stages/Asiatic impasse, but is based on another analytical principle that contrasts the full-blown forms of the tributary mode in the Chinese world with the peripheral forms of this same mode in the Mediterranean/European region. The full-blown form is visibly stronger and stable from its beginnings, while the peripheral forms have always been fragile, resulting in the failure of the successive attempts by the imperial centre to levy tribute, in contrast to its success in the Chinese empire.

The great pre-modern regionalisations and the centralisation of the tributary surplus

Nowadays, the term 'globalisation' is used in various ways, often vague and ambiguous. Moreover, the phenomenon in itself is considered as a given and unavoidable, an expression of the evolution of reality that is claimed to be ineluctable. Phenomena similar to modern globalisation, which for the first time in history concerns the entire world, are to be found in more ancient times. However, these only concerned the large regions of the old world, the so-called pre-Colombian Americas being isolated and unknown by the former (as well as by the latter). I will call these globalisations 'regionalisations'.

I describe all these phenomena with one common criterion: that of organising command over the surplus of current production at the level of the whole region (or of its world) by a central authority and the extent of centralisation over that surplus used by that authority. This in turn regulated the sharing of access to the surplus that it commanded.

The regionalisations (or globalisation) concerned could be inclined towards homogeneity or polarisation, according to whether the redistribution of the surplus was subjected to laws and customs that aim expressly at one or other of these objectives, or they could be produced by deploying their own logic.

The centralisation of tributary surplus

In all the pre-modern systems (the old regionalisations) this surplus appears as a tribute, and in the modern (capitalist) system as profit for capital or, more precisely, the rent of dominant oligopolistic capital. The specific difference between these two forms of surplus is qualitative and decisive. Levying tributary surplus is transparent: it is the free work of the subjugated peasants on the land of the nobles and a proportion of the harvest creamed off by the latter or by the State. These are quite natural, non-monetary forms and even when they assume a monetary form it is generally marginal or exceptional. The levying of profit or rent by dominant capital is, in contrast, opaque as it results from the way the network of trade in monetarised goods operates: wages of workers, purchases and sales of the means of production and the results of economic activities.

Taxation of tributary surplus is thus inseparable from the exercise of political power in the region (large or small) where it operates. In contrast, that of capitalist surplus appears to be dissociated from the exercise of political power, apparently being the product of the mechanisms that control the markets (of work, products, capital itself). The (pre-modern) tributary systems were not applied over vast territories and large numbers of people. The level of development of the productive forces typical of these ancient times was still limited and the surplus consisted essentially of what was produced by the peasant communities. The tributary societies could be split up, sometimes to the extreme, with each village or seigniory constituting an elementary society.

The fragmentation of tributary societies did not exclude them from participating in broader trade networks, commercial or otherwise, or in systems of power extending over greater areas. Elementary tributary systems were not necessarily autarchic, even if most of their production had to ensure their own reproduction without outside support.

The emergence of tributary empires has always required a political power capable of imposing itself on the scattered tributary societies. Among those in this category were the Roman, Caliphal and Ottoman empires in the Europe/Mediterranean/Middle East region, the Chinese empire and the imperial states that India experienced on various occasions during its history. This emergence of tributary empires in turn facilitated the expansion of commercial and monetary relationships within them and in their external relations.

The tributary empires did not necessarily pursue the political aim of the homogenisation of conditions in the region controlled by central power. But the laws and their usages governing these systems, dominated by the political authorities to which the functioning of the economy remained subordinated, did not in themselves create a growing polarisation between the sub-regions constituting the empire.

History has largely proved the fragility of tributary empires whose apogee was short – a few centuries – followed by long periods of disintegration, usually described as decadence. The reason for this is that the centralisation of the surplus was not based on the internal requirement necessary for the reproduction of the elementary tributary societies. They were very vulnerable to attack from outside and revolts from within, by the dominated classes or provinces, such as they were. Evolutions in the different fields, of ecology, demography, military armaments, the trade in goods over long distances, proved to be strong enough to turn this vulnerability into catastrophe.

The only exception – but it is a vital one – was that of the Chinese empire.

The peasant question at the heart of the opposition between the European and Chinese development paths

The Mediterranean/European path and the Chinese path diverged right from the beginning. The stability of the full-blown tributary mode involved a solid integration of the peasant world into the overall construction of the system and thus it guaranteed access to land. This choice has been a principle in China from the beginning. There were sometimes serious infringements in its implementation, although they were always overcome. In contrast, in the Mediterranean/Europe region, access to land was radically abolished when the principle of private ownership of land was adopted. It became a fundamental and absolute right, with the installation of capitalist modernity in its European form.

Historical capitalism, which was the result, then proceeded with the massive expulsion of the rural population and, for many of them, their exclusion from the building of the new society. This involved large-scale emigration, which was made possible by the conquest of the Americas, without which its success would have _en impossible. Historical capitalism became a military and conquering imperialism/capitalism, of an unprecedented violence.

The path followed by capitalist development in China (before it submitted to the conquering imperialism of the second half of the 19th century) was quite different. It confirmed, instead of abolishing, the access to land by the peasantry as a whole and opted for the intensification of agricultural production and the scattering of industrial manufacturing in the rural regions. This gave China a distinct advantage over Europe in all fields of production. It was lost only later, after the Industrial Revolution had successfully proceeded to shape modern Europe.

Accumulation by dispossession is a permanent feature in the history of actually existing capitalism

The ideological vulgarisation of conventional economics and the cultural and social 'thinking' that goes with it claims that accumulation is financed by the 'virtuous' savings of the 'rich' (the wealthy owners), like the nations. History hardly confirms this invention of the Anglo-American puritans. It is, on the contrary, an accumulation largely financed by the dispossession of some (the majority) for the profit of others (the minority). Marx rigorously analysed these processes, which he described as primitive accumulation, such as the dispossession of the English peasants (the Enclosures), that of the Irish peasants (for the benefit of the conquering English landlords) and that of the American colonisation being eloquent examples. In reality, this primitive accumulation was not exclusively taking place in bygone and outdated capitalism. It continues still today.

It is possible to measure the importance of the accumulation through dispossession – an expression that I prefer to that of primitive accumulation. The measure that I am proposing here is based on the consequences of this dispossession, and can be expressed in demographic terms and in terms of the apparent value of the social product that accompanies it.

The population of the world tripled between 1500 (450–550 million inhabitants) and 1900 (1,600 million), then by 3.75 during the

20th century (now over 6,000 million). But the proportion of the
Europeans (those of Europe and of their conquered territories in
America, South Africa, Australia and New Zealand) increased from
18 per cent (at most) in 1500 to 37 per cent in 1900, to fall gradually
during the 20th century. The first four centuries (1500 to 1900) correspond to the conquest of the world by the Europeans; the 20th
century – continuing through to the 21st century – to the 'awakening of the South', the renaissance of the conquered peoples.

The conquest of the world by the Europeans constitutes a
colossal dispossession of the Native Americans, who lost their
land and natural resources to the colonists. The Native Americans
were almost totally exterminated (a genocide in North America),
reduced, by the effects of this dispossession and their over-
exploitation by the Spanish and Portuguese conquerors, to a
tenth of their former population. The slave trade that followed
represented a spoliation of a large part of Africa that set back the
progress of the continent by half a millennium. Such phenomena
are visible in South Africa, Zimbabwe, Kenya and Algeria, and
still more in Australia and New Zealand. This accumulation by
dispossession characterises the state of Israel, which is a colonisation still in progress. No less visible are the consequences of
colonial exploitation among the peasantry subjected by English
India, the Dutch Indies, the Philippines and of Africa, as evinced
by the famines (the famous one of Bengal, those of contemporary
Africa). The method was inaugurated by the English in Ireland,
whose population – formerly the same as that of England —is
still only a tenth of that of the English, reduced primarily by the
organised famine in the 19th century.

Dispossession not only affected the peasant populations, which
were the great majority of peoples in the past. It also destroyed
capacities for industrial production (artisanal and manufacturing)
of regions that once and for a long time had been more prosper-
ous than Europe itself: China and India, among others (the developments described by Amiya Kumar Bagchi, in his last work,
Perilous Passage, provide indisputable proof of this).

It is important here to understand that this destruction was not
produced by the 'laws of the market', European industry – claimed
to be more 'effective' – having taken the place of non-competitive
production. The ideological discourse does not discuss the political

and military violence utilised to achieve it. They are not the 'canons' of English industry, but the cannons of the gunboat period. These won out because of the superiority – and not inferiority – of the Chinese and Indian industries. Industrialisation, which was prohibited by the colonial administration, did the rest and 'developed the under-development' of Asia and Africa during the 19th and 20th centuries. The colonial atrocities and the extreme exploitation of workers were the natural means and results of accumulation through dispossession.

From 1500 to 1800, the material production of the European centres progressed at a rate that was hardly greater than that of its demographic growth (but this was strong in relative terms for that era). These rhythms accelerated during the 19th century, with the deepening – and not the attenuation – of the exploitation of the peoples overseas, which is why I speak of the permanent accumulation by dispossession and not 'primitive' (i.e. first, preceding) accumulation. This does not exclude that the contribution of accumulation financed by technological progress during the 19th and 20th centuries – the successive industrial revolutions – then took on an importance that it never had during the three mercantilist centuries that preceded it. Finally, therefore, from 1500 to 1900, the apparent production of the new centres of the capitalist/imperialist world system (western and central Europe, the United States and, a late arrival, Japan) increased by 7 to 7.5 times, in contrast with those of the peripheries, which barely doubled. The gap widened as had never been possible in the history of all humanity. During the course of the 20th century, it widened still further, bringing the apparent per capita income to a level of 15 to 20 times greater than that of the peripheries as a whole.

The accumulation by dispossession of centuries of mercantilism largely financed the luxuries and standard of living of the governing classes of the period (the *ancien régime*), without benefiting the popular classes whose standard of living often worsened as they were themselves victims of the accumulation by the dispossession of large swathes of the peasantry. But, above all, it had financed an extraordinary reinforcement of the powers of the modern state, of its administration and its military power. This can be seen in the wars of the revolution and of the empire that marked the junction between the preceding mercantilist epoch and that of the subsequent industrialisation period. This accumulation is therefore at the origin of the two major transformations that had taken place by the 19th century: the first Industrial Revolution, and the easy colonial conquest.

The popular classes did not benefit from the colonial prosperity at first; in fact not until late in the 19th century. This was obvious in the tragic scenes of the destitution of workers in England, as described by Engels. But they had an escape route – the massive emigration that accelerated in the 19th and 20th centuries, to the point that the population of European origin became greater than that of the regions to which they emigrated.

Is it possible to imagine two or three billion Asians and Africans having that advantage today?

The 19th century represented the apogee of this system of capitalist/imperialist globalisation. In fact, from this point on the expansion of capitalism and 'westernisation' in the brutal sense of the term made it impossible to distinguish between the economic dimension of the conquest and its cultural dimension, Eurocentrism.

The various forms of external and internal colonialisms to which I refer here (for more details see *From Capitalism to Civilisation*) constituted the framework of accumulation by dispossession and gave substance to imperialist rent, the effects of which have been decisive in shaping the rich societies of the contemporary imperialist centre.

The Chinese itinerary: a long, calm river?

The preceding reflections concentrated on the Middle East/ Mediterranean/Europe region. This region was the scene of the formation of the first (tributary) civilisations – Egypt and Mesopotamia – and, later, of its Greek market/slavery periphery. Then, as from the Hellenistic period, it saw successive attempts to construct tributary empires (Roman, Byzantine, Caliphal, Ottoman). These were never really able to become stable and they experienced long and chaotic declines. Perhaps for this reason conditions were more favourable to the early emergence of capitalism in its historical form, as a prelude to the conquest of the world by Europe.

The itinerary of China was extremely different. Almost from the start it became a tributary empire that was exceptionally stable, in spite of the moments when it threatened to fall apart. Nevertheless, these threats were always finally overcome.

Phonetic writing, conceptual writing

There are various reasons for the success of the construction of tributary centralisation throughout the Chinese world. Chinese authors, who are not very well known outside their country (like Wen Tiejun), have proposed different hypotheses, depending on the geography and ecology of their region. They emphasise the early invention of intensive agriculture, associated with a population density that gradually became considerably greater than that of the Mediterranean/Europe world. It is not our purpose here to open up debate on these difficult questions, which have been barely studied much up until now because of dominant Eurocentrism. Personally, I would insist on the very long-term effects of the Chinese adoption of conceptual writing.

Phonetic writing (alphabetical or syllabic), invented in the Middle East, gradually became that of all the languages of the Mediterranean/European region and the Indian sub-continent. It is only understandable by those who know the meaning of the words pronounced in the written language, and it requires translation for the others. The expansion of this way of writing reinforced the differences between the languages and consequently the forms of identity that were based upon them. This constituted an obstacle to the expansion of regional political powers and therefore to tributary centralisation. Then, with capitalist modernity it created the mythology of the nation/state that was linguistically homogenous. This persists – and is even reinforced – in contemporary Europe and is thus an obstacle to its political unification. The obstacle can only (partially) be overcome by adopting a common language, foreign for many, whether it is the languages of the empires inherited by modern states (English, French and Portuguese in Africa, English in India and up to a point Spanish and Portuguese for the peoples of Latin America), or the business English that has become the language of contemporary Europe.

The Chinese invented another way of writing which was conceptual and not phonetic. The same character described an object (like a door) or an idea (such as friendship) and can be read with a different pronunciation: 'door' or *'bab'*, 'friendship' or *'sadaka'* by readers who are respectively English or Arab. This form of writing was an important factor promoting the expansion of the imperial power of the Chinese world at the continental level. It was a world whose population was comparable to that of all the Americas from Alaska to the Tierra del Fuego in Argentina and of Europe from Portugal to Vladivostok. The conceptual way of Chinese writing enabled phonetic reading in the different languages of the sub-continent. And it is only recently that, through generalised education, the Mandarin language of Beijing is becoming the (phonetic) language of the whole Chinese world.

China was five centuries ahead of Europe

The image of the Chinese trajectory as being the course of a 'long, calm river' is certainly somewhat forced.

Until the introduction of Buddhism in the first centuries of the Christian era, ancient China was constituted of multiple tributary formations, organised in principalities and kingdoms that were often in conflict. There was, nevertheless, a tendency to unifying into one single empire which had its early expression in the writings of Confucius, five hundred years before Jesus Christ, in the Warring States period.

The Chinese world then adopted a religion of individual salvation, Buddhism – although it was mixed with Taoism – following the example of Christian Europe. The two societies – feudal, Christian Europe and imperial, Buddhist China had striking similarities. But there were also important differences: China was a unified, political empire which rose to remarkable heights under the Tāng dynasty, while feudal Europe never achieved this. The tendency to reconstitute the right of access to land each time that it seriously deteriorated in China contrasted with the long-lasting fragmentation of European feudal property.

China freed itself from religion, in this case Buddhism, as from the Sōng period and definitively with the Ming. It therefore entered into modernity some five centuries before the European renaissance. The analogy between the Chinese renaissance and the later European one is impressive. The Chinese 'returned to their roots' of Confucianism, in a free, rational and non-religious reinterpretation, like that of the European renaissance that invented a Greco-Roman ancestor to break with what the Enlightenment described as the religious obscurantism of the Middle Ages.

All the conditions were then met to enable the modern Chinese world to accomplish remarkable progress in all fields: the organisation of the state, scientific knowledge, agricultural and manufacturing production techniques, rational thinking. China invented secularism 500 years before it developed in Europe. Modern China put forward the idea that it was man who made history, a notion which later became a central theme of the Enlightenment. The impact of this progress was reinforced by the periodic correction of dangerous drifts towards the private appropriation of land.

The stability of the economic and political organisation of China constituted a model for the development of the productive forces based on the continued intensification of agricultural production, which was in striking contrast with the model of historical European capitalism based on the private appropriation of agrarian land, the expulsion of the rural population, massive emigration and the conquest of the world associated with it. The model of this European capitalism was that of accumulation by dispossession, not only primitive but permanent (the other aspect of the polarisation inherent in capitalist globalisation). China was launched on a path that could have led to a capitalism of a different kind, closed up on itself rather than conquering. The prodigious expansion of commercial relations associated with the levying of tribute and not separated from it, show that this possibility did exist. But this association made the evolutionary process relatively slow compared with that of a Europe in transition towards full-blown capitalism.

For this reason China kept its advance – in terms of the average productivity of social work – over Europe until the Industrial Revolution of the 19th century.

As I said before, the Enlightenment in Europe recognised this advance of China, which it saw as a model. However, neither the Europe of the Enlightenment of the mercantilist transition period, nor, later on, Europe of the full-blown capitalism of the

19th century, managed to overcome the fragmentation of the kingdoms of the *ancien régime*, then of the modern nation-states, to create a unified power capable of controlling the centralisation of the surplus tribute, then capitalist surplus, as China had done.

For their part, Chinese observers clearly saw the advantage of their historic development. A Chinese traveller, visiting Europe in the aftermath of the French/Prussian war of 1870, compared the state of the continent to that of the Warring States, five hundred years before Jesus Christ!

The decline of China, caused by a combination of the exhaustion of the model of the intensification/commercialisation of agricultural and rural production, together with European military aggression, was relatively short. It did not cause the break-up of this continental state, although the threat was apparent during the decline. Some of the essential characteristics of the Chinese revolution and of the path it took after its victory, in the successive Maoist and post-Maoist moments, should be seen in this perspective of an exceptionally long duration.

Capitalism: a parenthesis in history

Dominant bourgeois thought has replaced the historical reality of capitalism by an imaginary construction based on the principle, claimed to be eternal, of the rational and egoistic behaviour of the individual. 'Rational' society – produced by the competition required by this principle – is thus seen as having arrived at the 'end of history'. Conventional economics, which is the fundamental base of this thinking, therefore substitutes the generalised 'market' for the reality of capitalism (and the 'capitalist market').

Marxist thought has been built up based on quite another vision, that of the permanent transformation of the fundamental structures of societies, which is always historical.

In this framework – that of historical materialism – capitalism is historical, has had a beginning and will have an end. Accepting this principle, the nature of this historical capitalism should be the object of continual reflection, which is not always the case in the ranks of the 'historical Marxisms' (that is, Marixism as interpreted by those who claim it). Certainly, one can accept the very general idea that capitalism constitutes a 'necessary' stage, conditions for socialism – a more advanced stage of vilisation. But this idea is too general and insufficient because it reduces 'capitalism – a necessary stage' to existing historical capitalism.

I shall sum up my reflections on this question in the following points, which will be developed in the following pages.

Accumulation through dispossession is a permanent feature in the history of capitalism.

Historical capitalism is, therefore, imperialist by nature at all stages of its development, in the sense that it polarises by the inherent effect of the laws that govern it.

From this it follows that this capitalism cannot become the 'unavoidable' stage for the peoples of the peripheries of the historical capitalism system that is necessary in order to create, here as elsewhere (in the centres of the system), the conditions for overtaking it by 'socialism'. 'Development and under-development' are the two inseparable sides of the historical capitalism coin.

This historical capitalism is itself inseparable from the conquest of the world by the Europeans. It is inseparable from the Eurocentric ideology which is, by definition, a non-universal form of civilisation.

Other forms of response to the need for 'accelerated accumulation' (compared with the rhythms of the accumulation of the ancient epochs of civilisation), a necessary premise for the socialism of the future, would have been 'possible'. This can be discussed. But these forms, perhaps visible in an embryonic way elsewhere than in the Europe of the transition to capitalism (in China, among others), have not been implemented because they have been crushed by the European conquest.

Thus, there is no alternative for human civilisation other than to engage in a construction of socialism, this in turn being based on the strategic concepts that must command the objective results produced by the globalised and polarising expansion of 'western' capitalism/imperialism.

The development of historical capitalism is based on the private appropriation of agrarian land, the submission of agricultural production to the requirements of the 'market' and, on this basis, the continuing and accelerating expulsion of the peasant population for the benefit of a small number of capitalist farmers, who were no longer peasants and who ended up by forming an insignificant percentage of the population (from 5 to 10 per cent). They are, however, capable of producing enough to feed all their country's population (well), and even export much of the surplus production. This path, started by England in the 18th century (with the Enclosures) and gradually extended to the rest of Europe in the 19th century, constituted the essence of the historical path of capitalist development.

It seemed very effective. But whether it is effective or not, can it be imitated today in the peripheries of the system?

This capitalist path was only possible because the Europeans had at their disposal the great safety-valve of immigration to the Americas, which we mentioned earlier. But this solution simply does not exist for the peoples of the periphery today. Moreover, modern industrialisation cannot absorb more than a small minority of the rural populations concerned because, compared with the industries of the 19th century, it now integrates technological progress – the condition of its efficiency – which economises the labour that it employs. The capitalist path cannot produce anything else than the 'slum planet' (which is visible in the contemporary capitalist Third World), producing and reproducing indefinitely cheap labour. This is in fact the reason why this path is politically unfeasible. In Europe, North America and Japan, the capitalist path – involving emigration outlets and the profits from imperialism – certainly created, rather belatedly, the conditions for a social compromise between capital and labour (particularly apparent in the period following the Second World War, with the welfare state, although this had already existed in less explicit forms since the end of the 19th century). The conditions of a compromise based on this model do not exist for the peripheries of today. The capitalist path in China and Vietnam, for example, cannot create a broad popular alliance, integrating the worker class and the peasantry. It can only find its social basis in the new middle classes that have become the exclusive beneficiaries of this development. The 'social-democratic' way is now therefore excluded. The inevitable alternative is one of a 'peasant' development model.

The question of natural resources constitutes a second decisive issue in the conflict of civilisation that opposes capitalism to socialism in the future. The exploitation of the non-renewable resources of the South for the exclusive profit of the consumption wastage of the North is also a form of accumulation by dispossession. The exchange of these resources against renewable goods and services jeopardises the future of the peoples of the South, who are being sacrificed on the altar of the super-profits of the imperialist oligopolies.

The destructive dimension of capitalism, at least for the peoples of the peripheries, makes it impossible to believe that this system can be sustainable and 'imitated' by those who seem to be 'backward'. Its place in the history of humanity is that of a parenthesis that creates the conditions for overtaking it. If this does not happen capitalism can only lead to barbarism, the end of all human civilisation.

The course of actually existing capitalism is composed of a long period of maturing, lasting over several centuries, leading to a short moment of apogee (19th century), followed by a probably long decline, starting in the 20th century, which could initiate a long transition to globalised socialism.

Capitalism is not the result of a brutal, almost magical apparition, chosen by the London/Amsterdam/Paris triangle to be established in the short period of the Reform/Renaissance of the 16th century. Three centuries earlier, it had experienced its first formulation in the Italian cities. The first formulas were brilliant but limited in space and thus crushed by the surrounding feudal European world. This is why, having been set back by successive defeats, these first experiences collapsed. It is also possible to discuss various antecedents to these, in the commercial towns along the Silk Route of China and India to the Arab and Persian Islamic Middle East. Later, in 1492, with the conquest of the Americas by the Spanish and the Portuguese, began the creation of the mercantile/slavery/capitalist system. But the monarchies of Madrid and Lisbon, for various reasons which we shall not go into here, were unable to give a definitive form to mercantilism which, instead, the English, Dutch and French were to invent. This third wave of social, economic, political and cultural transformations was to produce the transition to capitalism in its historical form that we know would have been unthinkable without the two preceding waves. Why should it not be the same for socialism: a long process, lasting centuries, for the invention of a more advanced stage of human civilisation?

The apogee of the system did not last long: hardly one century separated the industrial and French revolutions from 1917. This was the century when these two revolutions were accomplished, taking over Europe and its North American offspring – as well as the challenges to them, from the Commune of Paris in 1871 to the 1917 revolution – and achieving the conquest of the world, which seemed resigned to its fate.

Could this historical capitalism continue to develop, allowing the peripheries of the system to 'overcome their backwardness' to become 'developed' capitalist societies like those in the dominant centres? If this were possible, if the laws of the system allowed it, then the 'catching up' by and through capitalism would have had an objective unavoidable strength, a necessary precondition to an ulterior socialism. But this vision, obvious and dominant as it seemed, was simply false. Historical capitalism is – and continues to be – polarising by nature, rendering 'catching up' impossible.

Historical capitalism must be overtaken and this cannot be done unless the societies in the peripheries (the great majority of humanity) set to work out systematic strategies of delinking from the global system and reconstructing themselves on an autonomous basis, thus creating the conditions for an alternative globalisation, engaged on the long road to world socialism. I will not take up this analysis here, as it can be read in my *Obsolescent Capitalism* (Annex IV). Pursuing the capitalist path to development thus represents, for the peoples of the periphery, a tragic impasse. This is because the 'developed' capitalism of some – the dominant minority centres (20 per cent of the world population) – requires the 'under-development' of the others (80 per cent of the world population). The impasse can thus be seen in all dimensions of social, economic and political life. And it manifests itself most strikingly in the agrarian question.

 6

Russia in the world system: geography or history?

The double collapse of Sovietism as a social project distinct from capitalism and of the USSR (now Russia) as a state calls into question all the theories that have been put forward both regarding the capitalism/socialism conflict and the analysis of the positions and functions of the different countries and regions in the world system. These two approaches – the first giving priority to history, the second to geography – are often exclusive of one another.

In the tradition of historical Marxism, and particularly in its predominant version in the former USSR, the only great problem of the contemporary world recognised as worthy of scientific treatment was that of the passage of capitalism to socialism. As from Lenin, a theory of revolution and socialist construction was gradually formulated, of which I will summarise the theses in the following terms:

Capitalism must finally be overturned throughout the world through the class struggle conducted by the proletariat.

The socialist revolution has started in certain countries (Russia, later China) rather than in others because the former constituted, for various reasons, the 'weak links' in the chain of world capitalism.

In those countries the construction of socialism is possible in spite of their late development.

The transition of capitalism to socialism will therefore evolve in and through the competition between the two state systems, some of which have become socialist, the others having (provisionally) remained capitalist.

In this type of analysis, history – which governs the social and political particularities that constitute the different societies in the modern world (including those of the 'weak links') – plays the key role, to the point that the geography of the world system, in which the various positions and functions of these societies are determined, is entirely subordinated to history. Of course, the reversal of history, overturning the 'irreversible socialism' on behalf of capitalism, must question the whole theory of the transition to socialism and its construction.

Geography, however, takes on another dimension in, for example, an analysis of the movement of modern history inspired by the fundamental principle of what one can call, to be brief, the current way of thinking within the world-system approach. What happens at the level of the whole (the world system) controls the evolution of the parts that compose it. The roles played by the Russian empire and by the USSR would therefore be explained by the evolution of the world system and this is what makes it possible to understand the collapse of the Soviet project. Just as the extremists among the historical Marxists only know the class struggle through history, there is an extremist interpretation possible of the world-system approach that virtually eliminates the class struggle because it is incapable of changing the course imposed on it by the evolution of the system as a whole.

I should also mention here that theories about the specificity of Eurasia and its particular place in the world system had preceded the formulation of the world system approach by several decades. Already in the 1920s the Russian historians (Nikolai Trubetzkoy and others) had put forward such proposals, which were then forgotten by official Soviet conformism, but they were resuscitated in recent years. I would be in favour of a synthesis of the two types of analysis, particularly as concerns the Russian-Soviet case, having in fact already defended such an approach, in more general terms, which I believe to be enriching for Marxism (see Amin 1992).

The world system between the years 1000 and 1500, was clearly composed of the three main blocs of advanced societies (China, India and the Middle East), to which can be added a fourth, Europe, whose development was extremely rapid. It was in this last region, which had been marginal until towards the year 1000, that the qualitative transformations of all kinds crystallised and inaugurated capitalism. Between Europe and eastern Asia – from the Polish frontiers to Mongolia – stretched the Eurasian land mass, whose position in the global system of the period largely depended on the articulation between the four poles of what I have called the system of the ancient world (pre-capitalist, or tributary, if my definition of their social systems is accepted).

It seems to me impossible to give a convincing picture of the birth of capitalism without taking into consideration at the same time the two sets of questions concerning: (1) the dynamics of the local transformations in response to the challenges confronted by their societies, particularly the dynamics of social struggles; and (2) the articulation of these dynamics in the evolution of the ancient world system seen as a whole, in particular the transformation of the roles of the different regions that compose it (and therefore what concerns us directly here – the functions of the Eurasian region).

If we are to take the global viewpoint into consideration and thus relativise the regional realities, we must recognise that the great majority of the civilised population of the ancient world was concentrated, until very late, in the two Asian blocs (China and India).

Moreover, what is striking is the regularity of growth of these two blocs, whose population of some 50 million inhabitants, two centuries before the Christian era, grew to respectively 330 and 200 million in 1800 and 450 and 300 million in 1850. These extraordinary increases compare with the stagnation of the Middle East, precisely from the Hellenistic period. The population of the latter probably attained its maximum – 50 million – at this time and then declined almost regularly, stabilising at around 35 million on the eve of the Industrial Revolution and European penetration. (It should be recalled that the population of Egypt, which had been from 10 to 14 million inhabitants at certain epochs of the pharaonic age, fell to two million in 1800, and that the decline of Mesopotamia and Syria was of the same order.) Comparison should also be made with the stagnation of barbarous Europe until the year 1000 (from 20 million two centuries before the Christian era, probably less than 30 million towards the year 1000), and then its population explosion (with 180 million inhabitants in 1800 and 200 million in 1850).

It is then easy to understand that Europe, when it became aware of itself, became obsessed with the idea of entering into relationships, if not conquering, this fabulous Orient. Until late in the 18th century the Chinese empire was, for the Europeans, the supreme point of reference, the society that was the most civilised, the best administered, with its technologies that were the finest and most effective (Étiemble 1972). Its power was such that it was only from the end of the 19th century that anyone dared to attack it. In contrast, India, which was more fragile, had already been conquered and its colonisation played a decisive role in Britain's progress. Fascination with the Far East was the main impulse of the European initiatives. However, the discovery and then the conquest of the Americas absorbed European energies for three centuries. The function of Eurasia must be seen in this perspective.

The Middle East, which I consider the region that was the heir of Hellenism (a synthesis of five cultures – Egypt, Mesopotamia, Syria–Phoenicia, Greece–Anatolia, Iran) constituted the third pole of advanced civilisation.

The intense trade between these three poles thus affected the dynamic of the ancient world. These silk routes, as they are called, crossed the southern region of Eurasia, central Asia, from the Caspian Sea to China, to the south of the Kazakh steppe, from Tian Shan and from Mongolia (Amin 1991).

Nevertheless the relative stagnation of the Middle East pole (for reasons that are not relevant to this study) ended in a gradual decline of its foreign trade. There were at least two important consequences. The first was that Europe became aware, as from the Crusades, that the Middle East was not a rich region to conquer for itself, but the zone to be crossed or bypassed to reach the really interesting regions of Asia. The second was that China and India diverted their sights from the West to the East, constituting the peripheries that really interested them in Korea, Japan, Vietnam and in Southeast Asia. The two eastern poles did not actively search for relations with the Middle East in decline and still less with Europe. The initiative was therefore taken by the Europeans. The Eurasian land mass and the ocean were the two main competing passages enabling the Europeans to enter into Asia.

Europe was, as we have already said, marginal until towards the year 1000. Like Africa – which remained so after the year 1000 – it was a region in which the people were not really settled, nor constituted in tributary state societies. But this poor periphery of the ancient system suddenly took off, within a particular structure that combined a peripheral feudal tributary form (the fragmentation of powers) and a European universalism of Roman Christianity. During its progress which was to conclude by becoming the centre of the capitalist and industrial world as from the 19th century, it is possible to distinguish successive periods which, in turn, define the roles that Eurasia was to play in the accelerated dynamism of the system.

The Crusades (1100–1250) were the first stage in this rapid evolution. Western (Frankish) Europe then sought to break the monopoly of the Middle East, the obligatory (and expensive) passage for its relationships with eastern Asia. This monopoly was in fact shared between Orthodox Christian Byzantium and the Islamic Arab–Persian Caliphate. The Crusades were directed against both these adversaries and not only the Muslim infidel, as is so often said. However, finally expelled from the region, the Europeans tried other ways of overcoming this obstacle.

The Crusades accelerated the decline of the Middle East, reinforcing still further the lack of interest of the Chinese in the West. In fact, the Crusades facilitated the 'turkisation' of the Middle East: the increased transfer of powers to Turcoman military tribes which were called in for that purpose and hence they prepared the simultaneous destruction of Byzantium and the Caliphate, which were succeeded, from 1450–1500, by the Ottoman empire.

Furthermore, the Crusades enriched the Italian towns, giving them the monopoly over the navigation in the Mediterranean and prepared their active role in seeking ways to bypass the Middle East. It is interesting to note that two major routes were opened up by Italians: Marco Polo, who crossed the Russo-Mongol Eurasian land mass and, two centuries later, Christopher Columbus, who crossed the Atlantic Ocean.

Eurasia entered into history at that time, between 1250 and 1500; that is, during the course of the second phase of this history. Its entry marginalised the ancient silk routes that linked the Middle East to China and to India by the southern part of central Asia, to the benefit of a direct Europe–China liaison, passing further to the north, through the Eurasia of the Genghis Khan empire (this was exactly the route of Marco Polo). In turn, it opened the secular struggle for the control of Eurasia between the Russians of the forest and the Turko-Mongols of the steppes. The formation of the Muscovite state, its liberation from the Mongol yoke, then its increased expansion through Siberia, its military conquest of the southern steppes up to the Black, Caspian and Aral seas and the Caucasus mountain range, and finally southern central Asia itself and Transcaucasia … such were the stages of this impressive advance.

This history bequeathed Eurasia with some special characteristics which strongly differentiated it from the European formations as well as those of China. It did not, as is said rather superficially, become (or remain) 'half-Asian' (the expression obviously being in a pejorative sense). In fact it is too far away from the Chinese model to be so described. But nor did it become constituted into a densely populated, homogenous state as gradually happened in Europe, with its absolute monarchies and then with its modern bourgeois nation states. The occupation of such a large area weakened such characteristics, in spite of the desire of St Petersburg, as from 1700, to imitate European absolutism. Also, in the Russian empire the relationship between the Russians and the Turko-Mongol peoples of the steppes was not the same as that developed by the Europeans in their colonisation abroad. The former did not 'exploit' the work of the latter, as the Europeans did in their colonies; it was a political power (Russian) that controlled the spaces occupied by both peoples. This was, in a way, perpetuated in the Soviet Union, where the Russians dominated in political and cultural terms but did not economically exploit the others (on the contrary, the flow of wealth went from Russia to central Asia). It was the popularisation by fashionable media that confused these profoundly different systems by superficially terming them both empires (see Amin 1992).

Eurasia did not, however, play the role of a passageway linking Europe to China except for a short period, between 1250 and 1500, at a stage, moreover, when Europe did not yet have sufficient absorption capacity to bestow on the transit role of Eurasia the financial brilliance that the maritime commerce had later on. From 1500, in fact, the Atlantic/Indian Ocean route replaced the long continental crossing. And it was not only a geographical substitution. On their westward way the Europeans 'discovered' America, conquered it, and transformed it into a periphery of their budding capitalism, a destiny that Eurasia had escaped and which it would not be possible to impose upon it. At the same time the Europeans had also learnt how to colonise Asian countries (transforming them into peripheries of world capitalism), starting with India, the Dutch East Indies and the Philippines, then Africa and the Middle East, which was done in different ways from those invented by the Russian expansion into Asia.

The maritime route re-marginalised Eurasia from 1500 until 1900 and even after that. The Russians responded to the challenge in an original, and in many aspects, a brilliant, way. Foursov remarked that in 1517, the monk Philopheus had proclaimed Moscow to be the third Rome. This observation is worth bearing in mind because, as it was made so shortly after the maritime route had been opened, it gave Russia an alternative perspective, an exclusive role in history. There were some, like Nikolai Berdyaev, for example, who believed that Soviet communism pursued this aim of the Messianic role for Russia in advancing the progress of all humanity.

Russia therefore built itself up from then on, to make an effective synthesis of retreating into itself and opening to the West. The former task, that of a self-centred construction, was therefore in complete opposition to the peripherisation of world capitalism. There was no equivalent to this except for the self-centred construction of the United States pursued since its independence until 1914, or even until 1941.

So there were two large spaces that organised themselves as self-centred continents, obeying one sole political power. There have been no others, except for China as from 1950. Nevertheless, one cannot but note the mediocre results obtained by Russia/ USSR compared with the brilliant ones of the United States. There is a conventional explanation for this which contains a lot of truth: the advantage of the United States not having a feudal heritage (an argument that I reinforce when I say that New England was not constituted as a periphery of capitalism). But it is necessary to add that, isolated on the American continent, the United States was free from the vicissitudes of European politics and had only one adversary – Mexico – which was too weak to be anything other than a prey, half of whose territory was taken away from it. On the other hand Russia was not able to avoid the European conflicts and had to deal with rivals from western and central Europe: it was thus invaded by the armies of Napoleon, had to endure the affront of the Crimean war and was then twice more invaded, in 1914 and 1941.

This continual interference in the history of Russia and that of Europe was at least in part the result of the Russian – then Soviet – choice not to close itself up in Eurasia but to remain, or to become, as modern – that is, as European – as possible. It was the choice of the St Petersburg empire, symbolised by the two-headed eagle, one of whose heads looked towards the West. But it was also the choice of the USSR, which infused its ideology into the traditions of the European workers' movement. Its total rejection of Slavophil and Eurasian ideologies, which had always survived in the Russian empire, despite its official pro-Western option, is an obvious consequence of this.

The Russian revolution does not seem to me to have constituted at all a less important phenomenon which would hardly influence the course of history, once the Soviet parenthesis was closed. I do not find any other convincing explanation for this revolution than by involving simultaneously history (the new contradictions introduced by capitalism) and geography (the position of Russia in the capitalist economic world).

For capitalism certainly introduced a new challenge to the whole of humanity, to the peoples of its advanced centres and to those of its backward peripheries. On this essential point, I remain completely Marxist. By this I mean that capitalism cannot continue 'indefinitely' as permanent accumulation and the exponential growth that it entails will end up in certain death for humanity.

Capitalism itself is ripe to be overtaken by another form of civilisation, more advanced and necessary, through the leap in peoples' capacities of action that accumulation has enabled (and which is a parenthesis in history) and by the ethical and cultural maturation that will accompany it.

The question that the Russians posed in 1917 is neither artificial nor is it the odd product of their so-called 'Messianic' or the particular circumstances of their country. It is a question that is now posed to the whole of humankind.

The only questions that have now to be answered are, in my opinion, the following:

Why did this need to overtake capitalism so strongly manifest itself here, in Russia, and then in China, and not in the advanced capitalist centres?

Why did the USSR fail to change this need into a lever of irresistible progressive transformation?

In responding to the first question I would say that the geography of the world system certainly played a decisive role. The Leninist formulation of the 'weak link' is, I think, a first effort to explain what, in that sense, Mao generalised for the peripheries of the system in the theory of the continuous revolution by stages, starting from the 'New Democratic Revolution'. It is an explanation that takes into consideration the polarisation produced by the world expansion of capitalism, even though it does it imperfectly, as can be seen today. I would say here that the Russia that believed itself to be 'starting the world revolution' was not a peripheral country. It had the self-centred structure of a centre, but a backward one, which explained the violence of the social conflicts that took place. I would also say that the second great revolution – that of China – developed in the only large country which was not well and truly 'peripherised' as in Latin America, the Middle East, India and Southeast Asia. It had never been colonised. Instead of the well-known Chinese Marxist formula – a country that is 'half-feudal, half-colonial' – I would replace it with another which I consider to be more correct: a country 'three-quarters tributary, one-quarter colonial', while the other peripheries are 'one-quarter tributary (or feudal if you prefer) and three-quarters colonial'.

The second question requires a response that starts by challenging the theory of the 'socialist transition' as has been sketched above. I think that this is inexact, both in terms of the history and the geography of capitalism. It is based on an under-estimation of the (geographical) polarisation of the centres and peripheries, and in a lack of recognition that it is not due to particular historical circumstances (the 'natural' tendency of capitalist expansion being to homogenise the world), but that it is the immanent result of this very expansion. It therefore does not see that the revolt of the peoples who are victims of this development (which is necessarily unequal) has to continue as long as capitalism exists. It is also based on the hypothesis that the new (socialist) mode of production does not develop within the old (capitalist) one, but beside it, in the countries having broken with capitalism. I would replace this hypothesis with the one that, in the same way that capitalism first developed within feudalism before breaking out of it, the 'long transition' of world capitalism to world socialism is also defined by the internal conflict of all the societies in the system between the trends and forces of the reproduction of capitalistic relations and the (anti-systemic) trends and forces, whose logic has other aspirations – those, precisely, that can be defined as socialism. Although it is not the place here to develop these new theses concerning the 'long transition', I felt it necessary to mention them as I think they explain the reasons for the failure of Soviet Russia.

We may conclude by posing the questions that can throw light on the debate concerning not only Russia but also the world system.

The Soviet failure is not due to Russia, nor to the 19th century, nor – as Foursov suggests – to the pre-St Petersburg Muscovite period. For Russia, as for any other country, going back in history makes no sense. It is more a case of freeing oneself from this superficial kind of exercise and looking at the future from the viewpoint of an analysis of the present and its new features compared with the past.

How to get out of capitalism, and go beyond it, remains the central question for the Russians, the Chinese and all the other peoples of the world. If the thesis of the long transition that is sketched out here is accepted, the immediate step is to deal with the challenge which confronts us all: building up a multipolar world that makes possible, in the different regions that compose it, the maximum development of anti-systemic forces. This implies for the Russians and for the other peoples of Eurasia (formerly of the USSR) not an illusory capitalist development but the reconstruction of a society capable of going beyond it. A series of problems arising from this study should consider whether the Russians or the Chinese will be able to do this in the immediate future, or whether other peoples will do it more easily.

This chapter is an edited version of a paper that was first published in 1998 as 'La Russie dans le système mondial', Review, *vol. XXI, no. 2, pp. 207–19.*

References

Amin, Samir (1991) 'The ancient world system versus the modern capitalist world system', *Review*, vol. 14, Spring/Summer, pp. 349–86

—— (1992) 'Capitalisme et système-monde', *Sociologie et Sociétés*, vol. 24, no. 2, pp. 181–202

—— (1996) 'The challenge of globalisation', *Review of International Political Economy (RIPE)*, vol III, no. 2, pp. 216–59

Étiemble, R. (1972) *L'Europe chinoise*, Paris, Gallimard

Trubetskoy, N.S. (1975) *N.S. Trubetskoy: Letters and Notes*, The Hague, Mouton

Trubetzkoy, Nikolai (1991) *The Legacy of Genghis Khan and Other Essays on Russia's Identity*, edited by Anatoly Liberman, Ann Arbor, MI, Michigan Slavic Publications

Vernadsky, George (1961) *A History of Russia*, New Haven, CT, Yale University Press

Index

#

Ending the Crisis of Capitalism or Ending Capitalism?

Samir Amin

Ending the Crisis of Capitalism or Ending Capitalism?

978-1-906387-80-8
2010
Paperback £16.95

With his usual verve and sharpness Samir Amin, renowned radical economist, explores the systemic crisis of capitalism leading to the 2008 financial collapse, lays bare the relationship between dominating oligopolies and the globalisation of the world economy and analyses the attempts by the threatened plutocracies of the US, Europe and Japan to impose domination on the peoples of the South through intensifying military intervention. The current crisis, he argues, is a profound crisis of the capitalist system itself, bringing forward an era in which wars, and perhaps revolutions, will once again shake the world.

Amin presents an alternative strategy for the way forward which, by building on advances made by progressive forces in Latin America, would allow for a more humane society through both the North and the South working together.

Eurocentrism
Modernity, Religion and Democracy:
A Critique of Eurocentrism and Culturalism

Samir Amin

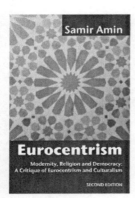

978-1-906387-78-5
2nd edition 2010
Paperback £12.95

Samir Amin, renowned radical economist,
takes on one of the great ideological
deformations of our time – Eurocentrism. He
defines and challenges the current historical,
political, economic and ideological order and
presents a sweeping reinterpretation that
emphasises the crucial historical role played
by the Arab Islamic world.

Since the first publication 20 years ago
of this original and provocative book,
Eurocentrism has become a classic of radical
thought. For this edition Amin has written
a new introduction and concluding chapter
to address contemporary concerns such as
Islamic fundamentalism which make his
arguments even more compelling.

'Samir Amin's fascinating book on the crucially important
subject of Eurocentrism ranges from the spread of Hellenism with
the conquest of Alexander the Great to the triumphs of imperialism
and transnational capitalism of the 1980s. While essentially thoughtful
and analytical, this study is quite rightly informed with outrage
against European arrogance and with sympathy for the non-European
victims on the periphery of the present system.'

Martin Bernal, author of
Black Athena: The Afroasiatic Roots of Classical Civilization
••

Lightning Source UK Ltd.
Milton Keynes UK
10 November 2010

162656UK00001B/8/P